A Little Hotel
On The Side

Translated by John Mortimer
from *L'Hôtel du Libre Echange*
by Georges Feydeau and
Maurice Desvallières

Samuel French – London
New York – Sydney – Toronto – Hollywood

ii

1. *This play is fully protected under the Copyright Laws of the British Commonwealth of Nations, the United States of America and all countries of the Berne and Universal Copyright Conventions.*

2. *All rights, including Stage, Motion Picture, Radio, Television, Public Reading and Translation into Foreign Languages, are strictly reserved.*

3. **No part of this publication may lawfully be reproduced in ANY form or by any means—photocopying, typescript, recording (including video-recording), manuscript, electronic, mechanical, or otherwise—or be transmitted or stored in a retrieval system, without prior permission.**

4. Rights of Performance by Amateurs are controlled by SAMUEL FRENCH LTD, 52 FITZROY STREET, LONDON W1P 6JR, and they, or their authorized agents, issue licences to amateurs to give performances of this play on payment of a fee. **It is an infringement of the Copyright to give any performance or public reading of the play before the fee has been paid and the licence issued.**

5. Licences are issued subject to the understanding that it shall be made clear in all advertising matter that the audience will witness an amateur performance; that the names of the authors of the plays shall be included on all announcements and on all programmes; and that the integrity of the author's work will be preserved.

   The Royalty Fee indicated below is subject to contract and subject to variation at the sole discretion of Samuel French Ltd.

   > Basic fee for each and every
   > performance by amateurs   Code M
   > in the British Isles

   In Theatres or Halls seating Six Hundred or more the fee will be subject to negotiation.

   In Territories Overseas the fee quoted above may not apply. A fee will be quoted on application to our local authorized agent, or if there is no such agent, on application to Samuel French Ltd, London.

6. The Professional Rights in this play are controlled by MARAGARET RAMSAY LTD, 14a Goodwin's Court, St Martin's Lane, London WC2.

The publication of this play does not imply that it is necessarily available for performance by amateurs or professionals, either in the British Isles or Overseas. Amateurs and professionals considering a production are strongly advised in their own interests to apply to the appropriate agents for consent before starting rehearsals or booking a theatre or hall.

ISBN 0 573 01616 X

A LITTLE HOTEL ON THE SIDE

This new translation first presented in the Olivier Theatre, at the National Theatre, on 9th August, 1984, with the following cast of characters:

Benoit Pinglet, a building contractor — Graeme Garden
Angelique Pinglet, his wife — Deborah Norton
Marcelle Paillardin, their next-door neighbour
Dinah Stabb
Henri Paillardin, her husband, an architect
John Savident
Maxime, Paillardin's nephew — Matthew Sim
Victoire, the Pinglets' maid — Judith Paris
Mathieu, the Pinglets' friend — Benjamin Whitrow
Head Porter — Bill Moody
Porters — Charles Baillie, Melvyn Bedford
Robin Lloyd, Paul Tomany
Violette ⎫ — Amanda Bellamy
Marguerite ⎪ Mathieu's daughters — Deborah Berlin
Paquerette ⎬ — Katrina Heath
Pervenchie ⎭ — Kelly Marcel
Bastien, the hotel manager — Michael Bryant
Boulot, the hotel porter — Robert Bathurst
Ernest, an actor — William Sleigh
Lady — Janet Whiteside
Chervet, a schoolmaster — Glenn Williams
Inspector Boucard of the Department
of Public Morality — Jeffry Wickham
First Constable — Paul Stewart
Second Constable — Peter Changer
Constables and Hotel Guests — Charles Baillie,
Melvyn Bedford, Judith Coke, Kate Dyson,
Robin Lloyd, Bill Moody, Shan Stevens,
Paul Tomany

Directed by Jonathan Lynn
Settings by Saul Radomsky

The action takes place in Paris just after the turn of the
nineteenth century

CHARACTERS

Benoit Pinglet, a building contractor
Henri Paillardin, an architect
Mathieu, the Pinglet's friend
Maxime, Paillardin's nephew
Boulot, a porter
Bastien, the hotel manager
Boucard, a police inspector of the Department of Public
   Morality
Ernest, an actor
Chervet, a schoolmaster
Angelique, Pinglet's wife
Marcelle, Paillardin's wife
Victoire, Pinglet's maid
Violette ⎫
Marguerite ⎬ Mathieu's daughters
Paquerette ⎪
Pervenchie ⎭
A Lady
Porters, Policemen, Hotel Guests

ACT I*

The office in the top floor apartment of M. Pinglet, a building contractor in Passy. A morning at the turn of the nineteenth century

From the windows we can see the tops of the buildings, roofs, the Eiffel Tower and some tops of tall trees. At the far end of the room french windows lead out to a narrow balcony with a railing. The door, DR, leads to Madame Pinglet's bedroom. At an angle UR is the door to an ante-room. UL, also at an angle, another door leads to Pinglet's bedroom. A large white trestle table is upstage in front of the windows, on it papers, plans, a ruler, a T-square, various pens and pencils and a directory

There should be enough room to pass between the table and the windows. A very high stool stands in front of the table. There is a kind of chest of drawers covered with samples of tiles and stone between the windows and the angled door UL, and a large work table covered with books and rolled-up plans against the wall on the L between the angled door and the forestage. On the work table are a blotter, a pen and an inkstand and a pot of flowers. A mirror hangs above it and above that there is a shelf on which there are more rolled-up plans. There is a sofa at an angle DL and a small writing desk UR between the windows and the angled door on the R. A portfolio stands against the wall between this door and Mme Pinglet's bedroom door. Above the portfolio there is a clock attached to the wall and to its right a bell-pull. Framed plans, tinted drawings and plaster models of cornices and ornamental mouldings decorate the walls. There is an armchair and three chairs. The armchair is against the wall on the L, a chair is between the writing desk and the angled door on the R, there are other chairs on each side of the windows. The locks on the doors are practical. The angled door on the R can be bolted from the outside. The windows are open and it is raining outside

As the CURTAIN rises, Pinglet, wearing a dressing gown as a jacket, is seated on a stool, working on a plan at the table C his back to the audience

Pinglet (*singing as he works*)
          Comes my love, with little fairy footsteps
          Comes my love, tiptoeing o'er the grass . . .
Mme Pinglet (*off*) Pinglet!

    Madame Pinglet enters DR carrying two sample rolls of material. She is a formidable and domineering lady

Pinglet (*singing*)
          Comes my love, to fill my soul with gladness!
Mme Pinglet (*harshly*) Pinglet!

---

*N.B. Paragraph 3 on page ii of this Acting Edition regarding photocopying and video-recording should be carefully read.

Pinglet (*without turning round*) There you are, Angelique, my dear heart!

Mme Pinglet My dressmaker's arrived.

Pinglet (*still not turning round*) Wonderful news! Your dressmaker's arrived. What am I expected to do? Stand to attention and sing the *Marseillaise*?

Mme Pinglet Stop working when I'm talking to you. (*She moves to the armchair and puts one roll on it*)

Pinglet (*aside*) And when she talks it cuts you like a knife! (*To his wife*) Angelique, my dear heart. You see, I have to get these plans done today. They're for a charming little villa I'm building. (*He rises and moves* UR *of the sofa*)

Mme Pinglet The charming little villa will have to wait its turn. (*She moves* L *and puts the other roll on the chair*)

Pinglet Of course, dear heart.

Mme Pinglet I've got these two fabrics. Which do you like best?

Pinglet (*looking at them*) Is it for the old sofa?

Mme Pinglet No! It is for my new tea gown.

Pinglet (*pointing to one of the patterns*) I rather like ... that one!

Mme Pinglet That settles it! I'll have the other. (*She picks up the second roll*)

Pinglet It wasn't much use asking me, was it dear heart?

Mme Pinglet It was a great deal of use. I know you have the most appallingly vulgar taste. You pointed out the one I wouldn't be seen dead in. (*She moves* DR *and pauses at the door*)

Pinglet (*aside*) Isn't she a little angel?

Mme Pinglet Get back to work then, Pinglet. Don't slack!

Mme Pinglet exits DR *with the material*

Pinglet Of course, Angelique. My darling heart! At once! (*He makes a face*) Ugh! That's no ordinary woman I've got in my house. ... It's the Emperor of Japan! (*He returns to his work table*) And to think I married her without my parents' consent. Of course, it was twenty years ago. If only we could've seen what they'd be like in twenty years' time we'd never have married them twenty years ago. I tell you, no son of mine will ever marry without my consent. If I ever have a son, which I won't. (*He shudders*) Well, with Madame Pinglet, would you?

There is a knock at the door

Come in!

Marcelle enters carrying a handkerchief. She closes the door

Pinglet, delighted moves to her

Welcome! Welcome, dear Madame Paillardin.

Marcelle Good morning, M'sieur Pinglet. Receiving in your dressing gown?

Pinglet We're next-door neighbours. We needn't stand on ceremony.

Marcelle I know. It's such a comfort. Your wife's not here?

Pinglet She is conducting high level negotiations with her dressmaker. How's your husband?

Marcelle I haven't the faintest idea.

Pinglet takes her hands and looks into her eyes. As he does, she turns away

Pinglet What's the matter?

Marcelle Nothing. (*She moves downstage, via* R *of the armchair*)

Pinglet (*following her*) Red eyes. You've been crying?

Marcelle Nothing much. Oh well. The same old story. (*She gives a massive sob and moves* L *to the end of the chaise*) A little difference of opinion. (*She sits on the chaise*)

Pinglet Is he being a brute?

Marcelle Of course he's not a brute. If only he were a brute there might be some faint hope for our marriage. He seems to find me considerably less attractive than a good drainage system. (*She sobs*) Please. Don't speak of it! It upsets me terribly. I must find your wife! (*She rises*)

Pinglet Through there. (*He points*) I think it's about time I had a few words with your husband. I might teach him to be a little civilized.

Marcelle (*moving towards the door*) Teach Paillardin to be civilized? You might as well teach a one-armed man to play the Beethoven Violin Concerto.

Marcelle exits DR *closing the door*

Pinglet (*watching her go, then excitedly*) What spirit! What a beauty! What a woman! My wife's always saying that I'm finished. If she means finished with her, for once we're in complete agreement. But am I finished with Madame Paillardin? I tell you. I haven't even started with Madame Paillardin! (*He fingers his moustache*) Look here. (*He points off* R) That wonderful girl is married to a kind of . . . lump of cold halibut. I mean, I can say it. He's my best friend. And your best friend's the one person in the world you can call a lump of cold halibut. If he weren't my best friend I might be rather rude about him. (*He leans on the end of the chaise*) Of course, it simply wouldn't do to try and seduce your best friend's wife. Well, not unless you were absolutely certain of success. And let's be brutally honest about this. I'm not certain of success. I mean, I wouldn't want to play a dirty trick on my best friend if all I got out of it was a slap in the face. Fine sort of friendship that would be. (*He returns upstage to his desk and unrolls a plan*) Now let's see what that lump of cold halibut has designed. (*Pause*) Can you believe it? (*He hold up the plan to the audience*) Limestone to support the weight of that beam. These architects! No practical sense whatever. (*He puts the plan down and prepares to work*) Paillardin couldn't build a rabbit hutch that wouldn't blow over in a high wind. All the same, he's got a beautiful wife.

Paillardin enters UR. *He closes the door and moves in a pace*

Pinglet looks furiously at the plan

Paillardin Morning, Pinglet, my dear fellow. Looks a little like rain, I think.

Pinglet Huh!

Paillardin What's the matter. You're not angry at all?

Pinglet No. Delighted to see you. I'm not in the least angry. What the hell do you think you're playing at here? (*He shows him the plan*)

Paillardin Playing at? Where?

Pinglet Limestone to support that beam!

Paillardin What do you expect me to use?

Pinglet Use rock. Use your head. Limestone's far too expensive. I suppose you think an entire villa can be supported by architectural theory . . .?

Paillardin (*moving to the armchair and sitting*) Oh, use what you like. Is my wife here?

Pinglet Through there. With mine. (*He rises and moves downstage*) And what *have* you been doing to her? Speaking as your best friend . . .

Paillardin Has she been complaining?

Pinglet She never complains! But you've only got to look at her, poor little thing. Eyes the colour of steak tartare. (*He sits on the chaise*)

Paillardin (*bored with the subject*) What's eating her? I'm a model husband. I haven't even got a mistress.

Pinglet You haven't got a mistress! Are you neglecting *all* your matrimonial duties?

Paillardin She thinks I'm not "loving" enough.

Pinglet Why? Aren't you? (*He picks up a cigarette from the table on his* R)

Paillardin What're things coming to? We live in a decadent age, Pinglet, old fellow. You're supposed to be "loving" to your wife nowadays. Are you "loving" to yours?

Pinglet Well, hardly. Look at her. I mean, my wife's been twenty years in the bottle. That's all right for wine. It doesn't do much to improve the quality of a wife. Mine's corked! (*He lights the cigarette*)

Paillardin You're perfectly right. Marcelle's a newer vintage. But she can have a distinctly acid flavour. You know what I think, my dear Pinglet?

Pinglet (*aside*) He thinks! An architect who thinks!

Paillardin I think that if you only get married for someone to go to bed with, well, you might as well take a mistress! (*He lights a cigarette*)

Pinglet What a delicate moral sense!

Paillardin No, but listen. I work hard. I spend all day climbing about on ladders and scaffoldings. At night I climb into bed for the peculiar purpose of going to sleep. My wife doesn't accept that! She says it shows a lack of respect for her finer feelings.

Pinglet Perhaps she has a point.

Paillardin (*sitting back, his legs crossed*) I don't care for hanky-panky, frankly Pinglet. I'm not a ladies' man. Never have been. Haven't got the taste for it. I find all that side of life, distinctly off-putting, somehow. That's why I got married!

Pinglet All right! Very well. You really are a glacier, you know. Ice cold and nothing moves you.

Paillardin Me, a glacier! Are you such a little volcano?

Pinglet You don't know me, do you? Beneath this calm, elegant exterior I am a cauldron! Boiling and bubbling with lava. Just at the moment I've got nowhere to erupt.

Paillardin (*laughing*) *You* a volcano!

Pinglet Well, you've got absolutely *no* lava!

Paillardin I haven't?

Pinglet And without lava a volcano's no more than a mountain with a boring little hole in the top.

Paillardin Now I remember what I came for . . . I suppose you couldn't lend me your maid?

Pinglet Victoire? What on earth do you want her for?

Paillardin She's for my young nephew, Maxime.

Pinglet Ah. That makes it perfectly respectable?

Paillardin Why can't you take anything seriously? Maxime's a swot who thinks of nothing but his philosophy.

Pinglet Philosophy when he's a schoolboy? What's he got left for his old age?

Paillardin The point is . . . he's starting his first term at the Lycée Stanislas to do his philosophy and I just haven't got a servant to take him there. You remember I gave mine the sack. She made blots with the furniture polish, all over my architectural drawings.

Pinglet (*aside*) They should've built the blots. They'd probably have stood up better.

Paillardin What did you say?

Pinglet I said, "If you really want the maid I'll get her!" Why don't you take the boy? After all, he's *your* nephew. (*He rises, moves* UL *and pulls the bell-pull*)

Paillardin No time. I'm busy all day . . . and tonight I'm sleeping away from home.

Pinglet Ah . . . ha . . . the glacier melts?

Paillardin Alone!

Pinglet You astonish me!

Paillardin (*moving* DL *and sitting at the desk*) Oh, my dear friend! I've got to spend the night in this horrible hotel. They allege it's haunted. (*Confidentially*) One hears strange sounds of knocking at night.

Pinglet Not the sort of thing you're used to at home.

Paillardin Certainly not! Knocking ghosts! Poltergeists. I'll wait till I see them, and then I won't believe in them! No. My mind's quite made up, it comes from the drains.

Pinglet Obviously.

Paillardin But the hotelier is asking to get out of his lease. The landlord's fighting the case and the Court's appointed me as the architectural expert! So I have to sleep there to decide the matter.

Pinglet That the knocking ghosts are only a touch of collywobbles in the central heating?

Paillardin Exactly. (*He rises and moves* UC *on his way to the door*)

Pinglet Henri! (*He moves towards Paillardin*) You haven't made up things with your wife.

Paillardin How can I? She's been blubbing away all day. She does nothing but complain that I take every opportunity to stay away from her. She doesn't understand that the architect comes before the husband.

Pinglet Oh my dear friend. Take care! Someone else may come before the architect.

Paillardin What can you mean?

Pinglet You're playing a dangerous game. Wives, particularly your wife, are creatures of sentiment. And if ever your wife deceives you . . . well, it'll be your own fault!

Paillardin My wife deceive me! She's not going to find a lover, just like that. That sort of thing only goes on in the theatre!

Pinglet Of course. Quite right! Only in the theatre. God speed you, Paillardin.

Paillardin All right.

Pinglet No. If your wife deceives you, I'll fall flat on my back! (*Aside*) So will she with any luck!

Paillardin moves to the door UR

Pinglet exits UL *to change from his dressing gown to a jacket*

There is a knock at the door

Maxime enters UR *with a book under his arm. He shuts the door. He is a serious boy, wearing spectacles*

Paillardin Oh, it's you, Maxime.

Maxime My dear uncle. (*He moves* DR *to the desk and searches the top, then moves to the* L *desk and searches the drawers*)

Pinglet enters UL

Pinglet Yes?

Maxime (*turning to Pinglet*) M'sieur Pinglet. Sorry to disturb you. I think I've lost the book I was reading. I may have left it here. (*He moves to the sideboard* UL *and finds the book on top*) Yes, here it is . . .

Paillardin What is it?

Maxime It's an extraordinarily interesting refutation of the philosophy of Descartes. It's by Carot, *The Treatise on the Passions.*

Pinglet And how to put them to practical use?

Maxime It's philosophy! It has no practical use, m'sieur.

Victoire enters and moves one pace in, leaving the door open

Victoire M'sieur.

Pinglet Yes, what is it?

Victoire Madame's asking for you.

Pinglet As usual.

Victoire She's with her dressmaker. She wants to consult your infallible bad taste.

Pinglet All right. All right. (*He moves* UC) Look here, Victoire. You're going to escort this young man to the Lycée Stanislas this evening.

Victoire (*looking at Maxime*) Delighted I'm sure.

Pinglet No one cares whether you're delighted. The point is . . . you will escort! (*To Maxime*) What time do you need escorting?

Maxime I have to be there at nine, Monsieur Pinglet.

Pinglet He has to be there at nine. Got that?

Victoire Delighted, m'sieur. (*She goes to the table and arranges the papers, plans, etc.*)

Paillardin (*to Pinglet*) I say, Pinglet. Thanks awfully.
Pinglet No trouble! (*He moves upstage to his desk*)

Paillardin moves a pace towards the door UR

Maxime moves to the sofa, sits and begins to read

Mme Pinglet (*off*) Pinglet!

Victoire moves to the desk DL

Pinglet Not a moment's peace! Off she goes again, like a fire alarm. Here I am, Angelique. Just coming, dear heart. (*To Paillardin*) My God, what a hornet that woman is! Buzzes round you the whole time and a terrible sting in the tail. Come along, Paillardin. Have you ever seen my wife at a fitting? It'll have you in stitches.

Pinglet and Paillardin exit R

Victoire What's the book, M'sieur Maxime?
Maxime This? Oh. *Treatise on the Passions.*
Victoire So what're you doing exactly?
Maxime Studying the entire subject of love. (*He crosses his legs*)
Victoire In that position? (*She moves to the chaise and lifts her skirt provocatively*)

Maxime ignores her

Victoire moves round behind him along the back of the chaise to the R *end*

Can I help? (*She sits beside him on the sofa*)
Maxime How can I study love with a woman sitting beside me?
Victoire (*leaning on the end of the chaise*) I might be able to make the odd suggestion.
Maxime Do you read Descartes, Mamselle Victoire? You can learn a lot from Descartes.
Victoire No. I only read tea leaves. You can learn a lot from them too.

Maxime returns to his book

(*Aside*) He's a nice boy. But on the timid side to look at him. (*She moves closer*) I bet you're a daring young man, aren't you, M'sieur Maxime?
Maxime (*reading aloud*) "We can distinguish between the passion of a lover for his mistress and that of a father for his children as we can distinguish between love and lust . . ." What did you say?
Victoire (*moving very close to him*) I bet you're ever such a daring young gentleman!
Maxime I certainly am not. I'm not daring at all. Not on any occasion. (*He reads*) "Nevertheless they are similar as they are both forms of love."
Victoire (*moving even closer to him*) If you're not daring what are you doing with your hand then . . .?
Maxime (*not looking up from his book and reading*) "A father desires nothing from his children that is not decorous and proper . . ."
Victoire Taking advantage of a girl in my position. To put your warm little hand where it never ought to go!

Maxime (*puzzled*) Where have I put my hand?

Victoire On my knee. You dirtly little devil, m'sieur! (*She takes hold of his hand and puts it firmly on her knee, holding it there tightly*) I bet that's all you think about at your age, isn't it? Putting your hands on girls' knees.

Maxime All I'm thinking about at the moment is philosophy. (*He returns to his book*)

Victoire Philosophy! (*She laughs*) Is that what they call it nowadays?

Maxime That's what they've always called it.

Victoire slides his hand up her leg

(*A little impatient*) Look, Victoire. How on earth am I going to learn about the nature of human love if you keep on interrupting me?

Victoire Just a touch. I could understand that. But keeping it there! (*She moves his hand and holds it firmly on her breast*) Your hot little hand. Such a long time. I'll have to complain to your uncle. Really I will!

Maxime gives a shocked look to the audience

Maxime (*puzzled*) What about?

Victoire What about? Don't act the innocent, M'sieur Maxime. Take it away this minute. Or I shall scream. I promise you! (*She holds his hand tightly on her breast*)

Maxime (*worried*) Please don't scream!

Victoire Try and stop me.

Maxime I can't read about Descartes with people screaming.

Victoire Stop me then!

Maxime How?

Victoire Block up my mouth.

Maxime It's impossible. You've got my spare hand.

Victoire Simply place your mouth firmly on mine, m'sieur. (*She takes him by the shoulders*) Before I raise the roof and bring the whole family in here running. (*She gets on top of him, forcing him to lean back and gives him a short kiss*) . . . Stop! You brute! You masterful brute! (*She puts her arms around his neck, pulls down his head and kisses him long and hard. His arms flap around, still holding the book. She leans back, pleased, while he gasps for breath*)

Maxime (*regaining his breath, aside*) What a curious sensation! Not altogether unpleasant.

Victoire (*angrily standing up and smoothing down her dress*) Don't you ever do that again young man. Or you'll be in serious trouble. (*She begins to move* R) Now I've got work to do. I shall see about escorting you later.

Victoire exits R, *leaving the door open*

Sound of shouting and quarrelling

Maxime She seems angry. I hope I haven't upset her. (*He blocks his ears and begins to read aloud*) "The affection honourable people have for their friends is of the same nature."

Marcelle, Paillardin, Pinglet and Mme Pinglet come in arguing

Paillardin For God's sake, Marcelle. What's eating you?

Marcelle What's eating me? I'm leading the emotional life of a stuffed aubergine!

Pinglet Stuffed! Surely not!

Mme Pinglet gives Pinglet a shove which sends him to the L *of the armchair, then closes the door* DR *and moves downstage*

Mme Pinglet Oh my dear. What will you say when you've had twenty years of so-called "married life"!

Pinglet (*moving downstage to confront Mme Pinglet*) Are you complaining? I've tried to make you happy.

Paillardin (*to Marcelle*) So have I.

Mme Pinglet
Marcelle } You've tried to make me happy?

Mme Pinglet advances on Pinglet. He backs behind the armchair. She slaps at him

Paillardin
Pinglet } (*together*) Yes I have.
Certainly.

Marcelle
Mme Pinglet } (*together*) You don't make me happy. Not in the least.
No you haven't. Not at all.

Paillardin
Pinglet } (*together*) Well, I've done my best. I still do.
Oh yes I have. I've tried.

Marcelle
Mme Pinglet } (*together*) Oh no you haven't.
You certainly don't.

They squabble amongst themselves

Maxime (*rising*) It's like trying to read Descartes in a parrot house!

Maxime exits rapidly UR

Marcelle What I ask myself is ... why on earth I'm married to this gentleman? He doesn't pretend to be a husband. He won't even go through the motions.

Paillardin (*stung by his wife's rebuke*) I say. That's a bit thick!

Marcelle He imagines that I got married for the pleasure of counting his dirty socks! He treats me like a laundry.

Mme Pinglet It's abominable.

Pinglet Do you?

Paillardin There's an element of exaggeration ...

Mme Pinglet (*to Paillardin*) You know, we've been married for twenty years, but if my husband treated me like that I'd ... I'd obliterate him!

Paillardin (*to Pinglet*) Would she?

Pinglet There's an element of boasting.

Mme Pinglet sits

Paillardin (*moving* DR *to his wife*) What do you want then? Do you want me to stay at home this evening? Do you want me to give up my professional life for the sake of half an hour's ... hanky-panky?

Marcelle Go on! Go and play with your drains. Whether you're here or there I find you equally distant.

Paillardin Oh, it's the same old story! (*He moves upstage and sits at the* R *end of the chaise*)

Marcelle I tell you, I'm going to start looking around. No one could stay an honest woman married to you.

Pinglet (*moving a pace nearer Paillardin*) In my opinion, Paillardin, old fellow. She's got a point!

Paillardin Don't you put your oar in! (*He retreats to the armchair and sits*)

Marcelle (*moving behind the chaise*) Just you watch out, that's all. One day someone else may give me all the treats I never get at home!

Paillardin You wouldn't!

Marcelle (*moving behind the armchair*) Why not? There're a lot of women much uglier than me who've found a little consolation.

Paillardin (*laughing*) You think I'd mind?

Marcelle Do you dare me? I won't be hard up for candidates.

Paillardin Go and find them then. Go on. Tell them to put up for election. (*He moves upstage*)

Mme Pinglet Paillardin. Don't provoke her.

Paillardin (*moving downstage*) She's provoking me! Oh, the happy, peaceful, glorious day when she finds her consolation! I only ask one thing of him, that he hangs on to her.

Marcelle (*moving* L *to Pinglet, furious*) Oh, M'sieur Pinglet!

Pinglet (*to Marcelle*) This is mad! (*To Paillardin*) You're mad! (*To the audience*) He's mad!

Marcelle Oh, that's what's the matter with him, is it? (*To Paillardin*) Remember. You wanted me to be unfaithful.

Paillardin (*rising and speaking to Marcelle*) I want it *passionately*! Good afternoon! (*He moves* UR *to the door*)

Mme Pinglet rises and follows to his L, *via below the chaise*

Marcelle moves DL

Mme Pinglet Look here, Paillardin. Give her a kiss. Make a fuss of her, why don't you?

Paillardin (*opening the door*) No, thank you very much. I'd rather step outside and kiss the Eiffel Tower. At least it wouldn't answer back.

Paillardin exits UR

Mme Pinglet (*following Paillardin*) Paillardin! Listen to me, Paillardin.

Mme Pinglet exits

Pinglet (*rising and moving to the door*) Henri! You're making a terrible mistake. You'll regret it, my best friend. I sincerely hope you'll regret it. (*He shuts the door and turns to Marcelle*)

Marcelle All right! Right! You heard it? You heard what he said? You heard it, didn't you? A fine way for a husband to talk! (*She sits on the sofa*)

Pinglet Yes. It was fine. (*He moves* L *of the armchair*) It was marvellous! Marcelle, I love you. (*He looks away* R *as she looks at him, then he looks at*

Mme Pinglet (*off*) Pinglet! Pinglet!

Pinglet (*falling on the floor*) And now I've woken up. (*To Marcelle, who is rising disengaging herself from his arms*) Marcelle, Marcelle. We haven't a moment to lose. Your husband's away tonight. You'll be free! And as for me, Pinglet! I'll be free as well.

Marcelle Yes?

Pinglet I'll call for you and we shall go ... (*he moves* L *in front of her*)

Marcelle Go where?

Pinglet Where? To paradise.

Marcelle Yes, but what's the address?

Pinglet The address. (*He pauses, then turns back to her*) I don't know yet. But I shall find out the address. I shall tell you the address, and we shall take ... our terrible revenge! Heads down! (*He jumps into the* L *desk chair and sits in a pose*)

Marcelle sits on the L *end of the chaise in a pose*

Mme Pinglet enters R, *closes the door and moves to the desk* DR

Mme Pinglet Delightful friends you cultivate, Monsieur Pinglet! (*To Marcelle*) Your husband really is a bit of a peasant, you know.

Pinglet What's he done now?

Mme Pinglet (*pulling roughly at a jammed drawer*) When I tried to use my most gentle persuasion, as a peacemaker, to save your marriage from the rocks, my dear Marcelle, can you imagine what he said?

Marcelle No.

Mme Pinglet "Take your long nose out of my business, you old hornet."

Pinglet (*delightedly*) He called you a hornet? (*Without conviction*) I can't believe it.

Mme Pinglet Neither could I.

Pinglet He said that to you? And you're so much older than he is.

Mme Pinglet (*sitting down*) I can't see what age has got to do with it. (*To Marcelle*) Oh, my dear. If my Pinglet ever behaved like that!

Marcelle What would you do?

Mme Pinglet No doubt about it. I'd find myself a lover.

Pinglet (*stifling his laughter*) Oh, Angelique. Dear heart. You wouldn't!

Mme Pinglet I certainly would.

Pinglet Where would she find a masochist?

Victoire enters UR *with a salver carrying letters*

Victoire Madame. A dress has arrived next door for Madame Paillardin.

Marcelle (*rising and moving to the door*) Just a little frock I had run up for myself.

Mme Pinglet Oh how sweet! And may your little frock make up for your disastrous marriage. Goodbye, Madame Paillardin.

Marcelle Goodbye. (*To Pinglet*) Goodbye to you, too.

Pinglet (*loudly*) Goodbye. (*Under his breath*) So it's all settled.

Marcelle Goodbye. (*She kisses his hand, then under her breath*) My husband has been asking for it.

Marcelle exits UR, *leaving the door open*

Pinglet (*cheerfully*) And I'm going to get it!
Victoire (*moving* DR *to Mme Pinglet*) Oh, Madame. Your post.
Mme Pinglet Very well. Leave it there. (*She indicates* L *end of the desk*)

Victoire puts the letters down and returns UL *of the armchair*

Pinglet Now . . . to discover a secret and mysterious rendezvous. Oh, what a
  fool I am. Of course! (*He hits the table as he thinks of it*)

Mme Pinglet opens a letter and reads it

  The Paris Directory. (*He picks up the directory from the desk and slams it
  down*)
Mme Pinglet Less noise, Pinglet. Victoire, (*she moves to the sofa with her
  letter*) I shall be dining out.
Pinglet (*aside*) Dining out! It's all going like clock-work. (*To Mme Pinglet*)
  Where will you be dining out, exactly, dear heart?
Mme Pinglet At my sister's. At Ville d'Avray.

Pinglet picks up the directory

  She's not getting any better.
Pinglet Nor are you.
Mme Pinglet What?
Pinglet I'll take a pew. (*He sits* DL *with the directory on his knees*)
Mme Pinglet She's not well. Read that, if you can.

Pinglet rises, puts the directory on the desk and moves R *to take the letter. He
returns* DL *to the desk and sits with the letter*

  And if I don't come back tonight, don't be disappointed.
Pinglet I'll try and bear it. As bravely as I can.
Mme Pinglet Have you got that in your head, Victoire? M'sieur will dine
  here alone.
Victoire Very well, madame.

  Victoire exits

Pinglet (*facing* DL *at the desk while leafing through the directory*) Haber-
  dashers . . . Hairdressers . . . Hingemakers . . . Hotels.
Mme Pinglet Ah, my dressmaker's sent in his bill.
Pinglet Ah . . . ha! Found it!
Mme Pinglet Found what?
Pinglet Found . . . it.
Mme Pinglet Have you?
Pinglet What?
Mme Pinglet What?
Pinglet I've found out what your dressmaker's sent in. His bill.
Mme Pinglet I know. I told you that!
Pinglet That's right!
Mme Pinglet You do say the most useless things from time to time.
Pinglet (*between his teeth*) Yes. Dear heart. Of course I do. Yes, of course.
  (*Aside, reading*) Hotel Summertime. No. Hotel of the Penguin and the

Fair Lady. What a ridiculous combination! The Grand Hotel of the Bicycle. The Hotel of the Heroic Fireman.

Mme Pinglet (*opening a second letter*) Good heavens!

Pinglet What?

Mme Pinglet Whoever sent these to *me*?

Pinglet What are they?

Mme Pinglet One ... two ... three ... circulars. From a hotel.

Pinglet A hotel?

Mme Pinglet Listen to this. It's perfectly shocking. "The Free Trade Hotel, two-two-oh, Rue de Provence. Specially caters for married couples. With or without each other"!

Pinglet (*rising*) With or without each other? It says that? In black and white?

Mme Pinglet See for yourself. (*She shows him the brochure*)

Pinglet (*taking it, delighted*) With or without each other. In black and white!

Mme Pinglet In my opinion it's a hotel for monkey business.

Pinglet I'm afraid you may be right. (*Aside*) Monkey business. Exactly what I need! (*Aloud*) "Rooms at all prices".

Mme Pinglet (*reading*) "Special reductions for season ticket holders"! It's disgusting!

Pinglet (*delightedly*) Disgusting! (*Aside, he moves* L) I shall get a season ticket. (*He puts the prospectus in his pocket*)

Mme Pinglet I can't imagine who would bombard me with salacious brochures.

Pinglet *I* certainly can't. (*He sits at the desk*)

Mme Pinglet tears up the other brochures and throws them on the floor

Victoire enters UR, *leaving the door open. She carries a card on a salver*

Victoire Madame. There's a gentleman to see you.

Mme Pinglet A gentleman?

Victoire His card. (*She hands a card to Mme Pinglet*)

Mme Pinglet Oh, it's Mathieu! Bless my soul. It's our old friend Mathieu.

Pinglet Mathieu? From Dieppe? He must be here on holiday. (*He rises*) Run along, Victoire. Show him up!

Victoire Yes, m'sieur. (*She turns aways to exit*)

Mme Pinglet Victoire. Clear up this mess.

Victoire gathers the torn up brochures, looking at them as she goes out

Mme Pinglet Mathieu's here. Our dear friend. (*She moves* CR *and tidies herself in the mirror*)

Pinglet Mathieu! Who was so kind to us when we took our holiday in Dieppe.

Mme Pinglet Put us up for two weeks. Lobster thermidore till it came out of our ears. And he's such a brilliant conversationalist!

Pinglet Of course. He's a barrister.

Victoire enters and holds the door open for Mathieu. He enters carrying a wet umbrella, hat, bag and gloves

Victoire In you go, m'sieur.

Pinglet moves to the L and Mme Pinglet to the R of Mathieu

   Victoire exits

Pinglet There he is! Come in then, dear old Mathieu.
Mme Pinglet What a wonderful surprise!

Mathieu kisses her hand

Pinglet How good of you to visit us!

Mathieu shakes Pinglet by the hand

Mme Pinglet (*indicating the sofa*) Do make yourself thoroughly at home!

Mathieu moves to the R of the chaise, then Pinglet moves to the R of Mathieu

Pinglet And let me have your umbrella. (*He takes the umbrella and hat and
   puts them in the stand*)

*At the same time Mme Pinglet moves above the chaise. Mathieu puts his bag
down at the R end of the chaise and puts his gloves in it*

   Poor old Mathieu. He's soaked to the skin!

Mme Pinglet moves to the L end of the chaise, still behind it

Mme Pinglet Of course he is. It's raining outside.

*Mathieu takes his coat off and sits on the R end of the chaise as Mme Pinglet
moves to the front of it and Pinglet moves to the armchair. He rises again,
seeing they are not seated. Seeing him rise, as they start to sit, they rise again.
Finally, all three sit*

Pinglet Now, to what do we owe this totally unexpected pleasure?
Mathieu Oh, my—my friends. I'm so—so ... I'm so—so.
Pinglet Only so-so?
Mathieu I'm so—so glad to see you. I'm ... mad ... mad!
Pinglet Surely he's exaggerating?
Mathieu I'm mad ... (*he kicks his leg and cries out*) Madame Pinglet's
   greatest admirer! (*To Mme Pinglet*) You're such a stupe ... stupe ...
   stupe ...
Mme Pinglet (*aside*) Is he working himself up to calling me stupid?
Pinglet Try and keep calm, Mathieu. Please try and keep very calm.
Mathieu Such a stupe ... (*he kicks*) ... endously generous woman!
Pinglet (*sitting on the sofa*) What on earth's the matter with him? (*To
   Mathieu*) Has something happened to you, old fellow?
Mathieu Wha ... wha ... wha ...
Mme Pinglet He wants a glass of water.

Pinglet rises to get one

Mathieu Wha ... (*he kicks, just missing Pinglet*) Whatever do you mean?
Pinglet It just occurred to me. ... It's hardly noticeable, of course, but

listening to you very carefully, can one just detect . . . a slight impediment in your speech?

Mme Pinglet And when we stayed with you in Dieppe, you hardly drew breath. No trouble then.

Mathieu It was s . . . summer then. During that fort . . . fort . . . fort . . .

Pinglet Fortnight?

Mathieu Two weeks. Every d . . . day was ho . . . ho . . . ho . . . ho . . .

Mme Pinglet |
Pinglet   } (*together*) Ho! Ho! Ho!

(*They join in, laughing appreciatively*)

Mathieu Not finished. Every day was ho (*he kicks up his leg and cries out*) Hot! In fine weather I can talk as well as anyone. But when it's raining. Pi . . . Pi . . . Pi . . . Pi . . . (*He crosses his legs*)

Pinglet We get the idea . . . (*He crosses his legs*)

Mathieu Pitilessly. Ma-ma, Ma-ma, Ma-ma-ma . . .

Pinglet Mother?

Mathieu Ma—my stutter comes back.

Pinglet The man's a walking barometer!

Mathieu When it's stormy . . . (*he turns to Pinglet confidentially*) . . . I can't fu . . . fu . . . fu . . .

Pinglet Steady on, old fellow! Ladies present.

Mathieu (*turning to Mme Pinglet, pelvis raised in an effort to get the words out*) Fu . . . (*he kicks*) Function!

Pinglet Not a word?

Mathieu Not a w . . . w . . . word!

Mme Pinglet But as a barrister it must be terribly difficult for you. What do you do if it comes on to rain when you're in court?

Mathieu I have to ask the judge if I can have a wee wee . . . a wee wee . . . wee . . .

Pinglet Does that make you feel better?

Mathieu A wee . . .

He gives a massive kick in Mme Pinglet's direction. She recoils and moves DL *to the desk, subsiding into a chair*

Week's adjournment.

Mme Pinglet Dear old Mathieu. You haven't forgotten us! Just arrived in Paris and your first call is on us.

Mathieu I remember so well your arse . . . your arse . . . your arse . . .

Mme Pinglet I can't believe my ears!

Mathieu Your asking me to stay.

Mme Pinglet Oh, I see.

Mathieu You said if I came to Paris I must stay under your roo . . . roof. You m . . . meant it?

Pinglet Of course we did.

Mme Pinglet The idea of you staying anywhere else! This *is* a treat for us.

Mathieu Dear Mme Pinglet. Always so ga . . . ga . . .

Pinglet She's not that old.

Mathieu Ga ... gracious.

Mme Pinglet And you too M'sieur Mathieu, always a gracious word.

Pinglet Eventually.

Mme Pinglet Well, stay as long as you like. Two days. Or three.

Pinglet Promise us you'll stay three days!

Mathieu N ... n ... n ... No!

Mme Pinglet We insist.

Pinglet Just to please us.

Mathieu No!

Mme Pinglet We really shall be quite cross if you go anywhere else.

Mathieu I shan't go anywhere else. I'm staying here for a m ... m ... m ... month.

Pinglet A month! (*He rises*)

Mme Pinglet (*politely*) It seems a little on the long side.

Mathieu Not at all.

Mme Pinglet We wouldn't want to impose on you to stay with us for a whole month.

Mathieu You're not.

Pinglet We're really delighted!

Mathieu rises and moves to the R of the chaise

(*Less enthusiastically*) Quite delighted. (*He moves* DL *to the* R *of Mme Pinglet*)

Mathieu takes off his jacket

Mme Pinglet (*aside to Pinglet*) A month's a bit steep. We only stayed with him for two weeks.

Pinglet But there were two of us. Two weeks each. It adds up, you know.

Mathieu I won't be a na-na ... na-na ... nuisance!

Pinglet A nuisance! (*He moves to pick up the wet coat and wipes the rain off the chaise. He puts it over the banister* UC *and returns above the chaise*) How could you be a nuisance? We've heaps of space. And you're travelling light. Just a bachelor with an overnight bag!

Mathieu Well, not exactly. I've brought a little surprise for you.

Pinglet Really! Angelique, my heart. This dear old fellow has got a little surprise for us!

Mme Pinglet (*rising*) A surprise! That's charming. He thinks of everything.

Victoire enters UR. *She stands to the* R *of the door*

Victoire I ought to warn you, madame. Someone's bringing up a trunk.

Mathieu Oh yes. It's mine.

A porter comes staggering in with a massive trunk on his back. He's panting, exhausted. He moves DCL

Porter It's like climbing the Himalayas.

Pinglet moves DL

Mathieu follows the porter

Victoire exits, closing the door

Mathieu Lay ... lay ... Oh, lay ...

Porter Olé to you, m'sieur. (*He turns to Pinglet*) A Spanish gentleman is he? (*He turns back to Mathieu*)

Mathieu Oh ... (*He kicks forcing the porter to back into Pinglet*) Lay it down.

Pinglet (*taking hold of the trunk*) M'sieur told you to lay it down.

Porter If you say so, m'sieur. (*He drops it on the floor*)

Mathieu How much do I owe you?

Porter (*assessing Mathieu*) Eighty sous.

Mathieu pays him

Mme Pinglet (*looking at it*) What an absolutely gigantic piece of luggage.

Pinglet It has a distinct look of Napolean's Tomb.

Victoire enters UR *and moves to the* L *of the door*

The porter moves above the chaise via the L *end and moves upstage counting his money*

We'll have it taken to your room. (*He calls*) Victoire! (*He moves to lift the trunk, fails and lays it down flat*)

Victoire (*moving in a pace*) Madame, there are more porters with more trunks.

The porter gives a sharp whistle and continues to move R

Pinglet
Mme Pinglet } (*together*) More? (*Mme Pinglet moves* DC)

Four porters enter, carrying trunks in descending size, Baillie first, then Tomany, Bedford and Lloyd. They move DLC, *put the trunks in a neat pile and return to the chaise area*

Mathieu Oh yes. They're all mi ... mine!

Mme Pinglet moves DR, *counting as she moves*

Mme Pinglet One ... two ... three ... four ...

Victoire and the first porter move R *of the door* UR

We're being taken over.

Mathieu It's my little surprise.

Mme Pinglet (*delighted*) Surprise. Words fail me.

Pinglet (*moving into view from behind the trunks*) I thought you were travelling light.

Mathieu Pinglet. I've got no change. Be a good fellow and see to these por ... por ... por ...

2nd Porter Of course we're poor, climbing half-way to heaven for forty sous.

3rd Porter I've done myself a permanent injury.

Mathieu Por ...

Mathieu kicks out, injuring Tomany who moves upstage, forcing Bedford to retreat to the L *end of the chaise*

Pinglet (*moving* R *to give Baille a coin*) There you are. Share that out among you.

Mathieu moves above the chaise

Why don't you go down to the kitchen. Get yourselves a nice glass of water . . . each. (*He moves upstage*)

Victoire ushers the porters out, leaving the door ajar

What sort of little surprise is it that needs five trunks?

Mme Pinglet So generous! (*She moves* DL *towards the trunks*) Well, we might as well open them . . .

Pinglet moves further upstage

Mathieu Why? (*He moves to the* R *end of the sofa to stop her*)

Mme Pinglet Why? For our surprise . . . (*She moves* UL *towards Mathieu*)

Mathieu No! (*He moves to the* UR *door*)

Mme Pinglet He wants to keep us in suspense! (*She moves to the* L *of Pinglet*)

Mathieu The surprise is cu . . . cu . . . cu . . .

Pinglet Custard glasses?

Mathieu Cu . . . (*He kicks out behind, then in front, missing Pinglet and Mme Pinglet who jump to the* L. *Instead he kicks the door, slamming it shut*) Coming!

Pinglet Missed me again.

Mme Pinglet M'sieur Mathieu. I can't wait to look into your trunks.

Pinglet I've known generous men in my time. But our dear old friend Mathieu's generosity is un-pa . . . un-pa . . . un-pa . . . Christ, he's got me doing it!

Mathieu Unparalleled?

Pinglet (*taking his hand*) Congratulations!

Mathieu I don't stutter for other people.

Victoire enters, knocking into Mathieu

Victoire Madame. There are some little girls just arrived by train. They've come up the stairs and they seem quite excited.

Mathieu Little girls. Are there four of them?

Victoire Probably. I wasn't counting.

Mathieu Then they're mine!

Victoire That's it then.

Victoire exits, closing the door

Mathieu (*to the Pinglets*) Hey p . . . p . . . presto. My surprise.

Mme Pinglet *Four* little girls?

Pinglet For us? I mean, I quite like little girls, in moderation, but . . .

Mathieu They're my daughters!

Pinglet No!

Mathieu When we met in the summer I was a bachelor. My wife had been dead for eight years.

Pinglet And presumably still is?

Mathieu Yes. My girls were in a convent. But they had to come out of the convent. A lot of the girls there had mum ... mum ... mum ...

Pinglet Mummys? And their's had passed away?

Mathieu Mum ... (*He gives a simple high kick forcing the Pinglets to lean away*) Mumps! So I went to collect them and I said to myself ... the poor Pinglets. They've never seen my g ... g ... girls. So I thought I'd give you a little surprise.

Mme Pinglet (*moving DR above the R desk*) Is *that* his surprise?

Pinglet (*following his wife*) I'd call it more of a shock.

Mathieu (*moving above the armchair*) So I came on ahead to announce them.

Mme Pinglet But the trunks?

Mathieu My little girls' bits and pieces.

Pinglet They're travelling heavy.

Sound of girls' voices

Probably moving in with their furniture. (*He moves R of the door*)

Mathieu Come along in girls. (*He opens the door*)

Mme Pinglet moves in front of the chair DR

Four girls enter (tallest first), carrying umbrellas and shoulder bags. They hook their umbrellas over Pinglet's L arm as they pass him, then form a line facing downstage, L of Mathieu. The smallest girl weaves in and out of the others to her place. Marguerite has a book. Pervenchie has a rag-doll and Paquerette has a lolly

Mathieu moves downstage to complete the line

Pinglet (*moving downstage*) He seems to have made the most of Madame Mathieu while she was with us!

Mathieu (*twitching his R foot*) Now my chilled ... chilled ... chilled ...

Pinglet ... blains?

Mathieu Chilled ...

Girls ... dren!

Mathieu Children. You've often heard me speak of Monsieur and Madame Pin ... P ... P ... Pin ... Pin ...

Girls Pinglet. (*They curtsey in unison*) M'sieur Pinglet. (*They curtsy*) Mme Pinglet. (*They curtsy*)

Mathieu There they are! Large as life. Surprise them! Give them a great big ha-ha, ha-ha, ha-ha. Hug!

Pinglet moves to put the umbrellas in the stand and then quickly moves behind the chaise as Pervenchie moves DR to Mme Pinglet and jumps onto her R hip. Paquerette jumps on her L hip. Mme Pinglet is forced to sit down and the other two girls rush up and surround her. The girls chorus "M'sieur Pinglet, Mme Pinglet" and embrace her

Mme Pinglet (*trying to escape from the girls*) Yes. Yes. They're totally charming but ... (*she fights her way DCR*) but it's an invasion.

The girls move to the chaise via DL and try to smother Pinglet with hugs, jumping on the chaise. As they finish, Pinglet emerges on his knees, glasses knocked off, from behind the chaise

The rain stops

Pinglet The biggest since the Franco-Prussian war!

Mme Pinglet We had no idea you'd gone in for daughters, in quite such a big way.

Mathieu (*pleased*) I am extraordinarily fertile!

Pinglet I suppose you'll be taking them straight to another convent. (*He rises*)

Mathieu (*moving to the front of the armchair*) No, no. I'm waiting for the mumps to disappear from theirs.

Pinglet But where are they all going to stay?

Mathieu Here, of course. (*He sits in the armchair*)

The girls sit on the chaise, biggest on the R end

Mme Pinglet Say that again?

Mathieu We're all going to stay here.

Pinglet I'm afraid that's unthinkable! Out of the question! (*He moves to the L of Mathieu*)

Mathieu But you both said . . .

Pinglet (*advancing on Mathieu*) We naturally say all sorts of idiotic things on holiday, when we're trying to be polite.

Mathieu Oh?

Pinglet You took me at my word. If you'd come alone, well, we'd have put up with you. Now you've gone too far. What do you think this is? A marine barracks!

Mathieu If I'd thought it was a marine barracks I certainly wouldn't have brought my children here! They are young girls, m'sieur!

Pinglet (*tapping him on the chest*) I'm astonished! Absolutely astonished. (*To Mme Pinglet*) What's he think we're doing, opening a house for stray orphans? This is Paris! Not the provinces. We don't all pile in together in mud huts.

Mme Pinglet It's all your fault, Pinglet! If you didn't scatter invitations around like confetti . . . (*she moves a pace, to the R of Mathieu*)

Pinglet It's not my fault. You said it was the least we could do. You said, "We've been here a fortnight. We've got to invite him."

Mme Pinglet (*giving Mathieu a sharp blow on his R shoulder*) Of course I invited you. I never thought for a moment he'd accept.

Pinglet (*giving Mathieu a sharp blow on his L shoulder*) And was it my fault that he turned up?

Mme Pinglet Of course it's your fault. If you'd just mentioned it in passing it might have all been forgotten. We'd have made the gesture. That was all that was needed. But no! You had to keep inviting him all the time, like a parrot with a one-track mind. "Come to our house, come to our house." (*She imitates a parrot, flapping her arms*) You insisted! Of course the poor fellow felt obliged to take you up on it. And bring the whole tribe with him.

Pinglet Don't find excuses for him. (*To Mathieu*) *Naturally* it's all my fault.

Mathieu (*standing up, surprised but resigned*) If I understand your drift Pinglet, you don't want us to stay with you!

Pinglet (*moving above armchair to* L *of his wife*) Got it in one! There's no room!

Mathieu (*rising*) Very well. Come along, children. Thank Monsieur and Madame Pinglet for their wonderful welcome.

The Pinglets retreat R *as the girls run across to them* en masse

Girls (*shaking the Pinglets' hands*) Thank you, m'sieur. Thank you for having us, madame.

Mathieu picks up his bag

Pinglet Don't mention it! (*To Mme Pinglet*) Angelique. My dear heart. You couldn't see if the porters are still getting their breath back in the kitchen. They could take away the impedimenta.

Mme Pinglet As soon as possible. (*She extricates herself, moves* UR *to the door and opens it wide with a significant look at Mathieu*)

Mme Pinglet exits as Marcelle enters. She pauses in the doorway as she sees the trunks

Marcelle All these trunks! It looks like a railway station.

Pinglet We're getting rid of them. Do come in, my dear.

Mathieu (*seeing Marcelle*) Madame!

Pinglet (*introducing them, delighted*) My dear lady. Allow me to present M'sieur Mathieu. The old friend you've heard us talk about so often.

Mathieu steps off the platform and kisses her hand. Marcelle looks over her shoulder at Pinglet

And his descendants! Madame Paillardin.

Girls Mme Paillardin. (*They curtsy*)

Pinglet gives a meaningful look at Marcelle who then moves DL *to the corner of the chaise. He then follows to her* R

Pinglet (*to Marcelle*) I've found exactly what we were looking for. You're still on?

Marcelle Absolutely!

Mathieu moves to the girls who crowd around him. They whisper

Pinglet Eight o'clock tonight at the corner of the Avenue du Bois and the Rue de la Pompe. Be in a cab with the blinds down.

Mathieu gives his bag to Pervenchie

I'll be wearing a white carnation and carrying *The Building Contractor's Gazette.*

Marcelle Why?

Pinglet So you can recognize me.

Marcelle But I know you already.

Mathieu (*moving above the armchair, to Pinglet*) After all that . . . where can I take my family?

Pinglet I'll see to you in a minute.

Marcelle (*under her breath, to Pinglet*) Where are we going?

Mathieu (*taking his coat from the banister and putting it on; aside*) If only I knew of a small, family hotel.

Pinglet (*taking a brochure from his pocket and reading*) Free Trade Hotel, two-two-oh Rue de Provence.

Marcelle repeats the address after hearing it and at the same time Mathieu, with one arm in his coat, takes a pencil from his pocket and writes on his cuff, speaking at the same time

Mathieu Thank you very much. Free Trade Hotel . . . two-two-oh Rue de Provence. Well then. Good afternoon.

Mme Pinglet enters with the porters. She moves towards C as the porters walk in a straight line to the trunks, pick up one each and exit via above the chaise

Girls Goodbye m'sieur. Goodbye madame.

The girls collect their umbrellas and exit

Mathieu (*collecting his hat and umbrella from the stand*) Goodbye, Madame Paillardin. (*He moves towards Pinglet*) You know where we'll be.

Pinglet Where?

Mathieu At the hotel.

Pinglet Oh yes. That's where you'll be.

Mathieu exits UR with Pinglet following him to the door

Off you go!

Mme Pinglet (*moving to the door*) Goodbye! I'm off to my sister's.

Mme Pinglet exits DR

Pinglet closes the UR door

Pinglet Oh, Marcelle. My little spring flower! If only you knew how happy I am. (*He laughs and moves to Marcelle, close to the chaise*)

Marcelle It's no laughing matter!

Pinglet Your husband's gone?

Marcelle Oh yes. And he hardly bothered to say goodbye. He'll be sorry.

Pinglet Listen. My wife's out to dinner. Your husband's gone. Before we make the supreme sacrifice, shall we have supper together?

Marcelle (*nobly*) What ever hardships are in store. I shall be brave!

Pinglet Eight o'clock at the corner of the Avenue du Bois . . .

Marcelle And the Rue de la Pompe.

Pinglet kisses her on the cheek. He turns his head away in ecstasy as Marcelle moves downstage of him to the R, wiping her cheek

Mme Pinglet enters R, wearing a coat, and goggles on her forehead and carrying a bag and a hat. Victoire is following her, carrying a tray. She stands to the R of the door

Mme Pinglet Are you leaving us, my dear?

Marcelle (*pausing and feeling her forehead*) I think I'm coming up for a cold.

Mme Pinglet Then you ought to be tucked up in bed.

Pinglet I quite agree.

Marcelle exits UR

Victoire moves DL and puts the tray on the desk. Mme Pinglet moves to the mirror and puts her hat on

What on earth's that?

Mme Pinglet Your dinner, of course. Victoire has to take young Maxime to the Lycée.

Pinglet moves to the tray for a look as Victoire moves UR and awaits orders

Pinglet My dinner?

Mme Pinglet What's the matter with you, Pinglet? Haven't you ever seen a dinner before? Go along, Victoire.

Victoire exits UR, closing the door

Mme Pinglet collects her umbrella from the stand

Pinglet (*moving UCL*) My dinner? I don't think I care for it. On second thoughts. I think I'll go to a restaurant.

Mme Pinglet (*heavily*) What!!!

Pinglet You're going to see your sister. I'm a bachelor and tonight I'll stand myself a rattling good meal!

Mme Pinglet In a restaurant? I forbid you to go to a restaurant!

Pinglet What's the harm in a restaurant?

Mme Pinglet You're a married man! Married men don't go to restaurants on their own. What would people at the other tables say?

Pinglet I suppose they'd say, "Oh, look. There's a married man having dinner on his own." What do you want them to say?

Mme Pinglet (*moving UR of the chaise*) The day you go trotting off to a restaurant on your own, I shall be beside you. Placing the order!

Pinglet (*faintly*) Everyone'll envy me, I'm sure.

Mme Pinglet Don't try to butter me up. Tonight you have your dinner here! On a tray.

Pinglet When're you going to stop treating me like a child?

Mme Pinglet When you grow up!

Pinglet (*moving below the chaise*) I don't care what you say. I shall go to a restaurant.

Mme Pinglet No, you shan't!

Pinglet I shall!

Mme Pinglet Shan't!

Pinglet Shall!

Mme Pinglet moves UR, *picks up a key from the corner of the cabinet nearest the door and returns* L *of the armchair. She brandishes the key in her* R *hand while holding the umbrella in her* L *hand*

Mme Pinglet Very well, my fine little fellow. I'll have to teach you a lesson. (*She takes the key out of the door*)
Pinglet (*trying to grab the key*) Give it to me!
Mme Pinglet (*holding the key away*) No.
Pinglet Will you give me that key!
Mme Pinglet (*holding her* R *hand in the air*) No! (*She uses her umbrella to hook his arm down*)
Pinglet I insist on having my key! A husband has every right to his own key!
Mme Pinglet (*transferring the key to her* L *hand*) No!
Pinglet Yes!
Mme Pinglet Don't argue!

She gives him a push under the chin with her R *hand. He falls back flat on his back on the carpet. She puts her goggles over her eyes and moves to the* UR *door, bumping into it*

> *Mme Pinglet exits, locking the door from the outside*

Pinglet (*getting up and rushing to pull open the door*) You haven't! You wouldn't! She would!
Mme Pinglet (*off*) Goodnight, M'sieur Pinglet. See you tomorrow.
Pinglet (*rushing to the desk* DR *and taking a key from the drawer*) Always keep a spare in the desk. (*He moves towards the* UR *door*)

The door bolt is shot

> She's shot the bolt!

> *Pinglet exits into the bedroom* DR *and then re-enters*

She's shot all the bolts! She's a methodical woman. (*He puts the key back down on the desk. He has an idea. He rushes to the window seat, opens it and produces a rope ladder. He shows it to the audience, then opens the window and throws it out. He then gets his hat, returns to the window seat, turns to the audience*) And with one bound Pinglet was free!

He waves his hat at the audience and jumps out of the window

CURTAIN

ACT II

The Hotel. Later the same evening

It is obviously a seedy and down-at-heel hotel with dirty tasteless wallpaper of a blue floral pattern and cheap furniture. It is 8.30 in the evening

The stage is divided into three parts. On the left-hand side, there is a hotel room. Against the wall, DL *is a little round table with a faded cover. Upstage to this, a door leads to a bathroom. At an angle, further upstage still is a chimney piece. Facing the audience, at the end there is a bed covered with an eiderdown, with flowery chintz curtains hanging from a mahogany ring screwed into the ceiling.* DR *there is a door onto the landing. The door opens inwards and away from the audience. A straw-seated chair is in the middle near the front of the stage. A zinc clock with a globe sits on the chimney-piece. On each side of it there are two candlesticks with candles and two painted porcelain vases with artificial flowers and plumes. There is a crocheted bed-cover on the eiderdown. On the bedside table is a jug, a glass and a sugar bowl*

The central part of the stage is the landing. The door of the above bedroom is DL. *Above it the number "10" is painted on the wall. Behind upstage, and at the far end facing the audience, is the staircase which leads up from below going from* L *to* R. *Facing the audience is another door with the number "9" above it. This room is on the level of the third step. From here on the stairs turn* R *and disappear up into the ceiling. The audience should be able to see the staircase going up as far as possible.* DR *is a board on which keys hang from numbered hooks. It is attached to the wall which separates the landing from the right-hand room. Below the board is a small table with drawers. On it there are flat copper candlesticks. One of them has been lit. A straw-seated chair is in front of the table. Beyond the table, further away from the audience, a door leads to the room on the* R. *This is number 11. The door opens inwards and away from the audience*

The third part of the stage is a large room, a kind of dormitory. On the L *between the door and the front of the stage, along the wall, is an iron bedstead with a small mirror above it. Opposite* DR, *are two more iron bedsteads facing the wall. A chair is in front of the first one. Upstage, a door behind the second bed leads to a bathroom. There is a window at an angle further upstage still. Below it is a fourth bed along the wall. At the far end, facing the audience on the* R, *a door leads to another bathroom (the door opens inwards). A chair is between the bed and the door. At the far end on the* L *there is a wooden bed with white curtains (just like the one in the room on the* L). *Behind the bedhead, which is on the* R, *there is a chair. A curtain-hook is on the wall near the bedhead. A bedside table is in front of it. A small round table with a cover is in the C of the room between the bed on the L and those on the R. There is grey wallpaper on the walls and ceiling*

The doors on the L and R of the landing should have practical locks with keys. It should also be possible to bolt the left-hand door from the inside

As the curtain rises the rooms on the L and R are in darkness. Only the landing is lit by two gas burners placed between the doors on the L and R and the stairs

Bastien, the manager, is sitting at a table on the R of the landing. He holds up two candles

Bastien Two candles (*He cuts them in half*) one plus one makes four candles ... (*he holds them up*). It may not sound much but in the thirty years I've been manager of this select establishment, man and boy, cutting the candles in half has made me six thousand francs. I'm not cheating them. Most of our clients prefer the dark.

Boulot, the under porter, comes rushing down the stairs, talking as he moves

Boulot Oh, my sainted aunt, M'sieur Bastien! If you'd seen what I've just seen!

Bastien I probably have. What was it?

Boulot I knocked, just like you told me, on the door of number thirty-two. I promise you, I took every precaution. And then a voice said, "Come in."

Bastien What did you do?

Boulot I went in.

Bastien This story is full of surprises.

Boulot Surprises! I was shocked, M'sieur Bastien. I was horrified! There was a naked woman in there!

Bastien Amazing!

Boulot Nakeder than naked! Like a shelled egg, M'sieur Bastien. And she said, "Porter!" she said. "Fetch me a pack of cards." Well, M'sieur Bastien. What could I do?

Bastien You could've fetched her a pack of cards!

Boulot A naked woman, paying patience? It's against nature!

Bastien Seems natural enough to me.

Boulot (*moving a pace downstage and speaking to the audience*) Life's totally different in the Provinces!

Bastien We've got to educate you, my young friend. We've got to make a Parisian out of you! When you've been here a couple of weeks you won't give a toss for a naked woman playing patience. "Madame," you'll say, "just pop your Black King on your Red Queen," and leave it at that. Now be a good lad and go and knock on number nine.

Boulot Number nine. What's she wearing in there?

Bastien Number nine's not a woman, Boulot. Number nine's a bone-headed schoolmaster who thinks he can enjoy our facilities and not settle our account. We'll keep his trunk and kick M'sieur Chervet out!

Boulot Is he the gentleman who's always threatening to blow people's brains out?

Bastien That's just his little joke.

Boulot But what if he blows *mine* out?

Bastien Then you come straight back here and tell me all about it. Jump to it, Boulot!

Boulot If you say so, M'sieur Bastien. (*He moves upstairs to two steps below number nine and turns to speak to the audience*) Not a very attractive assignment! (*He knocks timidly on the door*)

Chervet (*off, furiously*) Come in, then, damn you!

Boulot (*leaping back, terrified*) I'd even rather play patience with the lady upstairs.

Boulot goes into number nine

Bastien (*rising*) When he's been here thirty years he'll have got used to it. (*He moves downstage*)

Sound of bell ringing

What've we got here? Not regulars!

Ernest, a down-at-heel actor, enters with a large blowsy lady on his arm. They move downstage to Bastien, the lady sniffing at a bad smell

Ernest Varlet! Varlet! There you are. Have you, by any conceivable chance ...

Bastien I don't answer to "varlet".

Ernest Sirrah ... (*during Bastien's speech, he too smells the drains*)

Bastien (*to the audience*) I suppose I answer to "sirrah". (*To Ernest*) Yes, M'sieur. We certainly have, m'sieur. (*In honeyed tones*) Just what m'sieur is looking for. A charming little love nest where you and madame can snuggle down and no questions asked. And what a delicious morsel madame is, if I may say so, m'sieur. A morsel for a monarch! M'sieur is clearly a man of taste and discernment.

Ernest I didn't ask for your opinion, peasant!

Bastien (*still smiling*) Understood, m'sieur. I'm the soul of tact and discretion. M'sieur's in luck's way tonight. Number twenty-two's available. (*He turns back to the desk and removes a key from the drawer, leaving it open*)

Ernest Is number twenty-two where the two old tarts from Pigalle always go?

Bastien (*returning to the L of Ernest*) Yes, m'sieur. But we'll put you in there with one. (*He gives Ernest the key*)

Ernest Insolent dog! This lady is a lady of breeding. She is a person of refined taste and genteel education, closely connected with the aristocracy. She is a woman of the world.

Bastien All right. We'll let you up there with one woman of the world.

Ernest You know who I am of course.

Bastien Of course I do. Who are you?

Ernest (*taking off his hat and giving a bow*) I am Ernest "Casanova" Couet. The great leading actor of the Theatre des Batignolles.

Bastien Casanova? The name's familiar ...

Ernest (*to his companion*) You see, my dear. My fame goes before me.

(*Under his breath to Bastien whilst pulling him* DL) To be absolutely frank
with you, and not putting on side or anything . . . she's a Duchess! (*He
puts on his hat*)

Bastien Is she now? Congratulations! All the more reason for taking her up
to number twenty-two. It was in that room that the Crown Princess of
Poland spent her wedding night with her majordomo. (*He moves to the
lady*) You'll be thoroughly at home there, madame.

Ernest (*moving* L *and under his breath to Bastien*) But doesn't a fellow pay
through the nose for a Princess's room?

Bastien What's that to you, m'sieur?

Ernest What do you mean, "What's that to me"? It's my money, isn't it?

There is a terrific noise from number nine

Chervet (*off*) Get out and stay out.

*Boulot shoots out of the door and moves downstairs to Bastien, speaking as
he comes*

Boulot Oh, M'sieur Bastien! He keeps saying he'll blow my brains out, and
he won't leave without his luggage! (*He returns to the bottom of the stairs*)

Ernest What are those noises off?

Bastien A customer leaving. (*He moves upstairs, nearly to the landing*)
Chervet! Come here a minute!

*Ernest follows Bastien to the first step. The lady follows to upstage of door ten.
Boulot moves below the hall window*

Chervet comes out of his doorway. He is furious

Chervet What do you *want*? (*He hooks a cane round Bastien's neck and pulls
him round to face him*)

Bastien You see the stairs? You see the front door? Be so very kind as to
deprive us of your company.

Chervet When do I get my luggage?

Bastien When you pay your bill.

Chervet Very well! I've got a friend or two in the department of Public
Morality. Perhaps you'll stop larking about with my luggage when the
police descend on you! (*He moves downstairs*)

Ernest
Lady } (*together*) Not the police *here*?

Chervet Certainly the police! (*He brings Ernest and his lady* DC) And I can
tell them a thing or two about this hotel.

Bastien follows them downstairs. Boulot remains on the first step of the stairs

Ernest
Lady } (*together*) What?

Bastien When you've quite finished, Chervet.

Chervet (*raising his cane to indicate Ernest*) I'm talking to this gentleman.

Ernest fences Chervet off with his own cane

Call this a hotel! (*He brandishes his cane at Bastien*) What a dump!
Deserves a skull and crossbones in the *Michelin*. And the fleas . . .

Bastien That's not true. We spend a fortune on flea powder!
Chervet (*threatening Bastien*) Flea powder! It chokes the guests and the
fleas adore it. Added to which the place is haunted ...
Ernest }
Lady } (*together*) Haunted?
Bastien Chervet! Put a sock in it!
Chervet Evil spirits! Knocking ghosts! Poltergeists.

Bastien tries to placate Ernest and his lady

Come here. (*He moves to the door of number eleven*)

*Ernest and his lady follow quickly. Bastien moves after them to the doorway of
the R room. Boulot is still on the first step*

That room's the worst. (*He points to the room on the R*) Jam packed with
ghosts every night of the week. It's so bad they turned it into a dormitory
for the staff, and now the staff are scared stiff to go in there.
Lady Oh, horrors!
Bastien Grossly exaggerated!
Chervet It's got so serious they're calling in an expert. True or not?
Ernest This is not place for "Casanova" Couet. (*He gives the key back to
Bastien*) You can dispose of number twenty-two!
Bastien M'sieur's not going?
Ernest M'sieur certainly is. Come, Duchess.

Ernest and his lady exit UR

Boulot moves downstairs

Bastien (*to Chervet*) Now look what you've done!
Chervet Not enough. (*To Bastien*) You haven't heard the last of me! (*He
moves to Boulot, gets him by the ear and throws him downstage*) There are
brains round here that need blowing out.

Bastien hurriedly enters room ten and slams the door shut

If anyone can find them.

*As Chervet exits muttering, Bastien re-enters the hall and moves a pace
upstage to shout at him*

Boulot is getting up from the floor

Bastien You'll get thrown out of worse places than this.
Boulot He's lost us two clients!

Bastien moves to the desk and replaces the key. Boulot moves to his R

Bastien Clients! Don't talk to me about clients. I'm sick of them. All the
same, I wouldn't have minded seeing how "Casanova" Couet made love
to a real live Duchess.
Boulot You'd never have seen that?
Bastien Why not?
Boulot They might not have asked you to join them.

Bastien Silly noodle! (*He gives him a small slap on the cheek*) I'd have seen them all the same.

Boulot How?

Bastien How? (*He sits at the desk and takes a drill from the drawer*) What a simple soul! (*He shows Boulot the drill*) You know what that is, noodle?

Boulot It's a drill! For making holes.

Bastien Exactly! When I fancy a person ... (*He turns the drill*) I get myself an eye-ful! Through a small but convenient hole in the wall.

Boulot No!

Bastien Oh yes! I've seen some of the most beautiful women in Paris ... with the naked eye! And all free, gratis and for nothing!

Sound of a bell ringing

Paillardin (*off*) Manager!

Bastien hurriedly puts the drill on the desk and closes the drawer

> *Paillardin appears on the staircase carrying a small bag. He moves* DC *as Bastien rises*

Paillardin Manager! Where's the manager?

Bastien (*firmly*) At your service, M'sieur.

Paillardin gives him his bag. Bastien puts it on his desk chair

> M'sieur is expecting someone? I know exactly what M'sieur's looking for. A charming little love nest where you and your madame can snuggle down and no questions asked.

Paillardin No! Thank you, no! I'm not expecting anyone. I am Paillardin, Monsieur Henri Paillardin. The learned architectural expert appointed by the commercial court.

Bastien Oh, m'sieur, I understand! The haunted chamber! It's a little nest of enchantment.

Sound of a bell ringing

> Jump to it, Boulot. A customer's ringing. Look alive now, my lad. One two, one two!

> *Boulot rushes upstairs, closes the door of room nine and exits* UL

Bastien (*to Paillardin*) Oh, yes, m'sieur. The ghosts honour us with their presence. Every night. Lively spirits they are too. They kick up the most terrible shindig. They crack the walls! They chuck the furniture about! Like removal men!

Paillardin That's quite enough! I can investigate perfectly well on my own.

Bastien begins to light the candles

> Now where is this eventful room?

Bastien The one on the right, m'sieur. If you'll allow me to light a candle. (*He lights a very small candle, indicates the door to number eleven and picks up Paillardin's bag*)

Paillardin Lead on, to the haunted chamber!

They both go into the room on the right. Bastien moves to the L and puts the bag on the downstage end of the upstage bed. He then stays in the doorway on the downstage side after Palliardin enters

Bastien Rather you than me!

Paillardin Seems perfectly peaceful.

Bastien The spirits are always quiet at this time of night.

Paillardin (*plugging his pun*) In low spirits, perhaps?

Bastien (*on whom this joke has no effect*) But just you wait.

Paillardin Wait until when?

Bastien Until midnight, of course. When the lights are all off. The spirits get up to their tricks then.

Paillardin (*plugging his joke painfully*) Probably just *high* spirits.

Bastien High spirits, eh? (*Getting the joke at last, he laughs dutifully*) M'sieur the learned expert is a wit! But m'sieur the learned expert shall see what he shall see. (*He gives Paillardin the candle*)

Sound of singing from above, one verse of "Take me where the ladies dance all night" (see page 45)

Paillardin What's that? The spirits tuning up?

Bastien No, m'sieur the learned expert. (*He puts the candle on the shelf*) Just some of the young men from the Galleries Lafayette getting a bit above themselves with the girls from the lingerie department. I'll go up and read the riot act.

Bastien exits from the room and moves to the base of the stairs

Paillardin (*opening his bag*) My cigars. My hair brushes. (*He unpacks, putting his combs and brushes on the c table*)

Bastien (*shouting up the stairs*) This is a respectable establishment!

Coke (*off*) Tell us another!

Bastien Some people come here to sleep.

Moody (*off*) That's not what we've paid for.

Dyson (*off*) Why don't you put a sock in it, then?

Bastien Put a sock in it. I'll teach you to put a sock in it! (*He begins to move up the stairs*)

Paillardin moves to the doorway

Paillardin I say, garçon.

Bastien Half a jiff, m'sieur the learned expert.

Paillardin returns into his room, leaving the door open

I'll be back in half a jiff.

Bastien exits upstairs

Pinglet and Marcelle enter UR and move to the hall. Pinglet is smoking an enormous cigar and is carrying Marcelle's bag

Pinglet (*to Marcelle*) He'll be back in half a jiff.

Pinglet (*looking around*) It seems a nice, quiet little hotel.

Marcelle (*looking around*) It's horrible! Where on earth did you find it?
Pinglet It may be a little lacking in style. But it's just exactly what we want! In an A1 de luxe establishment we'd certainly be recognized. I don't suppose we'll meet any of our friends here.
Paillardin (*sneezing in his room*) Tishoo! (*He takes out his nightgown and slippers and puts them on the upstage end of the bed*)
Pinglet Bless you!
Paillardin (*taking off his hat*) Thank you very much!
Pinglet Don't mention it. (*To Marcelle, tenderly*) And who cares about the hotel?

Pinglet and Marcelle move downstage a little and then move to the R

We're together, darling Madame Paillardin . . .

Bastien enters UL and moves downstairs to the L of Pinglet

. . . and that's all that matters. (*He stops and sniffs*) Christ! What an extraordinary smell of drains. The plumbing could do with a little attention. Oh good. Here's the lackey.

Paillardin goes into the bathroom at the end of his room, taking a candle with him. His room is in darkness

Bastien At your service, m'sieur. (*In a servile manner*) I know exactly what m'sieur's looking for. A charming little love nest where you and madame can snuggle down and no questions asked . . . And what a delicious morsel madame is, if I may say so, m'sieur. A morsel fit for a monarch! M'sieur is clearly a man of taste and discernment.
Pinglet How dare you speak to me like that! This lady's my wife.
Bastien No!
Pinglet Yes.
Bastien No!
Pinglet Yes!
Bastien No. M'sieur's carrying the suitcase.
Pinglet (*aside*) A psychologist. (*He gives Marcelle her bag. To Bastien*) Have you a little something available on this floor?
Bastien More than a little something, m'sieur. A luxuriously appointed salon which we delight in calling . . . number ten. (*He takes the key out of the drawer and lays it on the top of the desk. Then he lights a candle and closes the drawer*) That's where the Crown Princess of Poland spent her wedding night with her majordomo.
Pinglet Perfect!

Bastien moves to the R door and enters. Pinglet takes his hat off and follows. Marcelle follows too. Bastien moves to downstage of the fireplace area

(*To Marcelle*) I told you it was a respectable hotel.

Bastien lights the candle on the downstage end of the fireplace. Pinglet puts his hat on the downstage bedpost, moves to the bed and bounces on it. Marcelle pauses just inside the doorway

Bastien There you are, m'sieur. (*He moves to the bathroom and opens the door*) Your bathroom.

Pinglet moves towards him

You're in luck's way tonight. Hot and cold running water . . .

Marcelle puts her bag down on the R end of the bed

. . . and our guests are cordially invited to partake of it.

Bastien exits into the bathroom to leave the candle there

Pinglet (*turning to face Marcelle*) Madame Paillardin.

She moves to him at the downstage end of the fireplace

May I call you Marcelle, darling?

Pinglet is about to embrace Marcelle as Bastien emerges from the bathroom. Marcelle sees him over Pinglet's shoulder

Marcelle Ssssh! He's still here.
Bastien Oh.
Pinglet (*turning and finding himself face to face with Bastien*) Aah!
Bastien Aah!
Pinglet Er—very well. I shall take this room.
Bastien (*closing the bathroom door*) Goodnight m'sieur. (*He moves to the C of the room and turns to Marcelle*) Madame.

Bastien exits to the hall, closing the door

Marcelle follows to check that he has gone, then turns to Pinglet who moves to her and they begin to embrace. Pinglet has one foot on the bed

Bastien, having picked up the key from his desk, returns to their room

Pinglet At last! (*He takes Marcelle in his arms*)
Bastien Your key.

Pinglet and Marcelle spring apart, Pinglet moving to the fireplace where he adopts a nonchalant stance. Bastien hands Pinglet the key, who places it on the mantelpiece

Bastien exits to the hall, closing the door

Paillardin comes out of his bathroom, crosses his bedroom and walks into the hall with a candle, startling Bastien

Bastien Aaah! M'sieur's not leaving us already?
Paillardin Just for a breath of fresh air.

Marcelle takes her hat off and puts it on the bed

Pinglet admires the picture over the fireplace

I'll have a beer in the cafe opposite. Back in half an hour.
Bastien Very good, m'sieur. M'sieur will find his candle waiting for him. (*He takes Paillardin's candle*)

Paillardin exits UR

Bastien is about to blow out the candle when he hears a noise from upstairs. He puts the candle down on the desk (upstage end) and rushes upstairs

Pinglet (*moving towards Marcelle, whilst still smoking his cigar*) Marcelle! (*He takes her in his arms*)
Marcelle Pinglet!
Pinglet Oh ... I'm no longer Pinglet to you. Call me Benoit!
Marcelle (*shrugging*) If you like. Why? (*She disengages herself and moves away*)
Pinglet It's my name of course. Benoit Pinglet.

Marcelle moves DL

Marcelle! Marcelle. (*He moves to her*) The terrible hour of vengeance on your appalling husband has arrived! You'll get your own back—on your own back! (*He tries to grab Marcelle, cigar in his mouth*)
Marcelle Look out! You're going to set me on fire!
Pinglet On fire with love! (*He catches her by the waist and turns her around*) I love you, Marcelle! More than anything in the world. (*He is puffing smoke in her face*)
Marcelle (*coughing*) It's like being cuddled by a chimney! (*She pushes him away*)
Pinglet Oh! (*He takes out his cigar and looks at it*) Pardon me.
Marcelle Can't you throw it away?
Pinglet (*doubtfully*) It cost me forty sous. I was planning to smoke it right down to the end.
Marcelle (*hurt*) So I take second place, to a forty sous cigar?
Pinglet (*moving to the fireplace*) You're right! When it's an affair of the heart, what does money matter? (*He throws his cigar into the coal scuttle, after a last puff and stands with his* L *hand resting on the mantelpiece as he surveys Marcelle*) And you're staggeringly beautiful!
Marcelle (*moving upstage a pace whilst removing her coat*) How do you like my dress? (*She puts her coat on the bed and twirls around*) Do you like me in puce?
Pinglet It's perfectly all right. In fact, yes. I like you in or out of puce!
Marcelle It came from the dressmaker this afternoon. You're the first person to see it on.
Pinglet The dress! What's the dress matter? The dress is nothing but the dish which contains the delicious little cutlet! (*With passion*) So far as I'm concerned, it might as well not be there. It's unnecessary. It doesn't add anything to your beauty. (*He moves to her, pulling at the back of her dress in an attempt to undo it*) We can get on perfectly well without your dress! I want you desperately, Madame Paillardin. (*He gets impatient and yanks at her dress*) Marcelle!
Marcelle (*struggling*) Oh, good heavens! What's got into you, Pinglet? M'sieur Benoit! Do please be careful! (*She moves away* L)
Pinglet (*moving behind her and holding her in his arms*) I want you! I've wanted you ever since you moved in next door and come in to borrow a

stick of sealing wax. I didn't want to give you the sealing wax, I wanted to give you ...

Marcelle (*extricating herself*) The champagne's gone to your head!

Pinglet Nonsense. (*He moves* R, *past the chair*) Everything's done me good! The miraculous Marcelle, the beautiful Beaujolais, the charming Chartreuse. The soothing cigar. My wife says smoking and drinking make me ill. Look at me! I'm in the pink! (*He taps his chest and wheezes*) I've never felt better in my life! (*He moves to Marcelle and draws her to him as he sits on the chair. The chair breaks. He falls to the ground. He shouts*) Stupid chair!

Marcelle (*bursting out laughing*) You look so funny!

Pinglet (*aside*) Now she finds me ridiculous.

Marcelle (*laughing*) You haven't done yourself an injury?

Pinglet (*getting up*) An injury? Of course not. I did it on purpose. I do a little tumbling at times. Just to amuse the ladies. Idiotic chair! (*He picks up the chair*) And it's the only one! (*He throws the chair out onto the landing*) Clear out! And don't come back. (*Aside*) Now then. Let's get on with it. (*He tries to take her in his arms again*) Marcelle!

Boulot enters UL *and moves down the stairs*

Marcelle (*pushing him away and laughing*) If only you could have seen yourself!

Pinglet (*put out*) Well I couldn't. I had to leave that to you.

Marcelle (*still laughing*) I looked round. And you suddenly seemed to have shrunk!

Pinglet It isn't really very funny!

Boulot sees the chair pieces and picks them up

Marcelle No, of course it isn't! (*She stuffs her handkerchief in her mouth to stop herself laughing*) You're absolutely right ... It's not ... funny ... at all!

Boulot It's the chair from number ten. Who put it there?

Pinglet (*swooping on Marcelle*) My dear Marcelle!

Boulot goes into Pinglet's room with the chair and starts back in surprise Marcelle and Pinglet spring apart

Boulot Pardon me! (*He stands in the doorway, holding the chair pieces*)

Marcelle ⎱ (*together*) Oh!
Pinglet ⎰

Boulot M'sieur. I didn't know this room was taken ... I'm just putting your chair back for you.

Pinglet (*furiously*) No! Take it away! I never want to see it again!

Boulot But m'sieur. It belongs in here.

Pinglet Not any longer. I've thrown it out. I've had quite enough of it! You and that chair. Get out, both of you! (*He pushes Boulot out onto the landing, closes the door and leans against the bedpost, exhausted*)

Boulot She's a bit of a morsel, that young lady. I wouldn't mind seeing more of her. (*He has an inspiration*) The drill. (*He moves towards the drill on the desk whilst still holding the chair*) Why not?

Bastien (*off*) Boulot! Boulot!
Boulot I'm coming. I'm coming.

Boulot exits UL *with the chair, leaving the drill untouched*

Pinglet (*anxiously*) My God! What a peculiar sensation.
Marcelle What's the matter?
Pinglet I'm not sure. It's a cold sweat! Now it's a hot sweat! Rising steadily.
It must be excitement. Nothing to worry about. (*He moves to Marcelle*)
Marcelle! We're alone at last. I wish you could see what's going on inside
me. I can feel my heart . . . my heart. Oh, my God! My heart's going pit-a-
pat! In an alarming manner!
Marcelle (*concerned*) You've gone terribly pale, Pinglet! Benoit! Are you all
right?
Pinglet Just feeling a little dickie. The ticker . . . and all that. (*His legs
collapse*)
Marcelle (*frightened*) Sit down, for heaven's sake!
Pinglet (*looking round desperately*) Where? The chair's gone.
Marcelle Sit on the table then. (*She helps Pinglet to the table* L)
Pinglet (*sitting on the table*) Oh, Marcelle! I'm terribly sorry. The happiest
moment of my life. And I'm not up to snuff! Better in a minute. (*He grips
his stomach and moans*) Oh . . . my God!

Marcelle moves UL *of the table and pours some water in a glass, then takes her
handkerchief out*

Marcelle Hang on. I'll get you something to drink. (*She starts to prepare
water and sugar*)
Pinglet (*in rueful despair*) It was the cigar. I told you it was the cigar. It
doesn't matter. Better soon. The cigar and the champagne. Me! And all I
usually drink is water . . . Oh, my God! (*He stands up and staggers to the
fireplace*)
Marcelle (*stirring the sugar in the water*) You poor thing! (*She moves to him*)
Pinglet I feel terrible. And my wife's not even here!
Marcelle (*bringing him the glass*) Do sit down!
Pinglet I can't! I've got to keep on the move. (*He moves towards the
bedroom door and turns*) I need fresh air.
Marcelle Then I'll come with you. (*She moves to him with the glass*)
Pinglet No! No, I've got to go it alone. Help. I'm suffocating!
Marcelle Oh dear—take your jacket off.
Pinglet Not now, Marcelle . . . Oh, I see.

She helps him off with his jacket and puts it on the bed

Oh, I'm sinking!
Marcelle Come along now. Brace up!
Pinglet (*with despair*) I feel very near the end. (*He leans against the wall,
downstage of the door*)

Boulot enters UL, *moves downstairs and picks up the drill*

Marcelle Don't say that! One can't be seen dead in this hotel! (*She wipes his
forehead with her handkerchief after wetting it in the glass*)

Boulot Now then. After all. Bastian does this all the time.

Marcelle moves to Pinglet and mops his brow with her handkerchief

(*Tapping the wall*) Where are we going to start drilling? There? That seems nice and yielding. (*He kneels with the drill opposite Pinglet's bottom and starts to turn it*)

Pinglet (*leaning back against the wall*) Oh, that feels so refreshing ... and beautiful, Marcelle.

Boulot Just a little spy hole ... down there ... and they'll be none the wiser!

Marcelle Better?

Pinglet Oh yes! Your touch ... is so exciting!

The drill is now through the wall. As it first touches him Pinglet wriggles with a sort of ecstasy

Boulot That's going in nice and easy.

Pinglet (*startled*) —Oh, my God!

Boulot is finding it harder to turn the drill

Marcelle What is it?

Pinglet A kind of pricking sensation in the lower ... the lower back.

Marcelle That's a good sign. It means the blood is draining out of your brains.

Pinglet (*giving a sharp cry*) Aah ... ah ... oh ... ah ... ouch!

Marcelle What did you say?

Pinglet (*hurling himself away from the wall*) Ouch! (*He leaps up and moves DR to the fireplace*) It's agony ... sudden agony!

Boulot What's the matter with it? (*He pulls the drill out and inspects it*)

Pinglet Ouch! Appalling sensation!

Marcelle (*moving to Pinglet*) What's the matter now?

Pinglet An indescribable pain. Just as though someone were trying to penetrate my ...

Marcelle Thoughts?

Pinglet No, not my thoughts, my lower back.

Marcelle It's a sort of seizure.

Boulot (*looking at the end of his drill*) Rising damp! (*He touches it*) It's red in colour. Must be the brick.

Marcelle You look terrible! Shouldn't we send for a doctor? (*She puts the glass on the mantelpiece, picks up her hat and fans him with it*)

Pinglet Just give me air. All I need is air. And a drink. (*He fans himself with Marcelle's hat*) A cup of camomile tea. (*He rushes to the door*)

Boulot (*getting on all fours to look through the hole*) Now let's have a little look-see.

Pinglet (*opening the door*) Lackey! (*He falls over Boulot's back*) What on earth are you doing down there?

Boulot Keeping my ear to the ground. I thought I heard m'sieur calling.

Pinglet Really? Listen. I need air. Show me to a garden, a terrace, even a little balcony!

Boulot Straight upstairs, m'sieur. Turn right. End of the corridor ...

Pinglet Thank God! (*He rises and begins to rush up the stairs*)

Boulot scrambles up and moves L of the bedroom door

Marcelle (*appearing at the door and speaking to Boulot*) And please bring
m'sieur a hot water bottle.
Pinglet Yes! That's what I want. A hotty! (*He carries on up the stairs, calling
to Marcelle*) You will wait for me!
Marcelle (*moving to the first stair*) Don't worry! (*She moves* UR *of Boulot*)
Pinglet The happiest day of my life. And I'm feeling dreadfully sick!

Pinglet exits UL *as Boulot puts the drill on the desk*

Marcelle (*to herself*) Poor Pinglet! (*To Boulot*) Quick. Camomile tea. Any
sort of tea. So long as it's camomile.
Boulot (*shrugging*) Everything's shut. Just a minute. That brute we just
chucked out next door! (*He moves upstairs as he speaks*) He was always
making tea.

Boulot exits into room nine

(*Off*) He'll have the necessary.

Marcelle returns to her bedroom and paces about anxiously

Marcelle What a chapter of accidents!

*Boulot returns downstairs with a tray and goes into room ten moving L of
Marcelle*

Boulot Here we are, madame! All the tackle.
Marcelle Put it down there. (*She indicates the small table* L)
Boulot (*putting the tray down*) Very well, madame.
Marcelle Are you sure the gentleman won't catch a cold, up there on the
balcony? He's in a most delicate state of health.
Boulot (*lighting the spirit lamp under the kettle*) Don't worry, madame! The
air is exceedingly balmy. Not a bit like this morning when it was raining
cats and dogs. Now it's a beautiful moonlit night. (*He winks at her*) A
night for lovers!

Mathieu enters UR *with his daughters, speaking as he walks. They all carry
umbrellas and bags. They move* DC

Mathieu Come along now, children. Come along . . .
Girls We're coming, Papa. Here we are, Papa.
Mathieu (*talking volubly*) Well, here we are and where's the porter? I mean.
I've never seen a hotel like this before. Anyone could just walk in off the
street. I mean, we might have been burglars so far as anyone knows. We
might have been cut-throats, footpads, murderers or confidence trick-
sters! Pickpockets even! Why have a front door bell if you leave the door
wide open!
Violette Oh, Papa! You're so eloquent! Anyone can tell it's stopped raining!

Mathieu moves DL. *The girls follow, in line, to his* R

Mathieu But I can't imagine why Pinglet recommended this place. (*He
smells the drains*) Perhaps it's gone downhill rapidly. All the same, it's

late. We'll stay one night. Not worth getting your trunks up, girls. We'll
find somewhere else tomorrow.

Marcelle (*to Boulot as the kettle boils*) Very well. You can go now.

Boulot stands

Don't forget the hot water bottle.

Boulot Certainly, Madame. (*He moves slowly to the door, looking admiringly
at Marcelle*)

Marguerite I like A1 de luxe hotels . . . with soft carpets and perfumed soap
in the bathrooms . . .

Violette So do I . . .

Paquerette So do I . . .

Pervenchie So do I . . .

Mathieu So do I . . .

Boulot moves into the hall, closing the door

Marcelle exits into the bathroom

Boulot moves downstage CR, *speaking as he moves and not noticing the
Mathieu family*

Boulot That poor invalid's lady friend is an absolutely charming morsel!

Girls *There's* the porter! (*They turn to him*)

Boulot My God. What do they think this is? A boarding school?

Mathieu Look here, porter. (*He pushes through the girls to Boulot*) This
place was recommended to me by M'sieur Pinglet.

The girls reform around Mathieu

Boulot M'sieur Pinglet. But of course! (*Aside*) Never heard of him.

Mathieu Now then. What accommodation can you offer for me and my
daughters?

Boulot (*aside*) His daughters! (*To Mathieu*) These are *all* your daughters,
m'sieur? (*Aside*) The fellow must breed like a rabbit.

Mathieu Look sharp about it. What can you show us?

Boulot (*looking at the keys on the desk*) Let me see now.

Boulot moves to the desk. They all follow

I'm never going to find enough rooms for . . . all of you. (*Aside*) I've got an
inspiration! The haunted room! Can't let that for love or money. (*To
Mathieu*) If you're not too finicky, m'sieur, I think I might have something
available. (*He lights a candle*)

Mathieu Lead us to it.

*Boulot moves to room eleven and stands inside the doorway on the upstage
side. The Mathieus follow, the girls waiting outside for their father to enter
first. Mathieu enters, then the girls in line, smallest first*

Boulot Here we are—the State Apartment.

Mathieu (*stopping dead in the* C *of the room, the girls likewise behind him*) It's
a barracks!

Boulot It's all we can offer, m'sieur. And with four girls and your good self it's very suitable. Look, five beds exactly.

Mathieu But a Papa can't sleep in the same room as his daughters. It's out of the question!

Boulot (*working his way through the girls to Mathieu*) M'sieur can hop into bed first and pull the curtains round him when the young ladies undress. And we can offer segregated toilet accommodation. (*He moves past Mathieu to below the bed*)

Girls (*to Mathieu*) Segregated toilet accommodation!

Mathieu I suppose we've got no choice.

Boulot None whatsoever, m'sieur.

Mathieu And how am I expected to pay for your State Apartment?

Boulot To *you* m'sieur. And seeing you come recommended by M'sieur What's-his-name. . . . What would you say to seven francs a night? All in.

Marcelle enters from her bathroom and moves to the C of her room

Mathieu Sounds reasonable. (*He takes his hat off*)

Marcelle What on earth's Pinglet up to? He's been gone for hours.

Mathieu (*to Boulot*) Very well, my man. We'll take the room. (*He puts his bag, hat, umbrella and coat on the bed*)

Girls Hooray.

All, except Violette, put their bags and umbrellas on their beds. Pervenchie puts her doll down

Boulot Excellent, m'sieur! (*He moves R of Mathieu, giving him the candle*) Goodnight, m'sieur. Sleep well, young ladies.

Girls Sleep well, porter!

Boulot exits into the hall, closing the door. He moves to the desk, pushes the chair in and begins to move towards the stairs

> *The Girls exit into their bathroom, leaving the door open. They remove their coats and leave them in there. Violette also takes her bag*

Marcelle Perhaps he's been taken poorly again! I'm beginning to worry about him.

Mathieu But I must have a candle for my girls.

Marcelle moves to the landing, leaving her door open as Mathieu does the same

Marcelle (*to Boulot*) I say, porter!

Mathieu I say, porter!

Marcelle (*turning to Mathieu*) M'sieur Mathieu!

Mathieu (*turning to her*) Madame Paillardin. Unless I'm very much mistaken.

Marcelle (*turning her back on Mathieu*) No . . . no . . . well . . . yes. As a matter of fact it is.

Boulot moves upstage, between them

Mathieu I had the pleasure of meeting you at the home of our mutual friends, the Pinglets.

On the right the Girls are making themselves at home

Marcelle Ah no. I mean yes. No. The pleasure was mine. Entirely.

Boulot (*surprised*) Amazing! They know each other.

Mathieu Well, what a lovely surprise. (*He moves to the door and calls*) Children!

Marcelle No, please, m'sieur. . . . Don't trouble your children.

Mathieu But of course. It's no trouble, madame! Come along, children. Who do you think I've found? Madame Paillardin.

Marcelle My God! He's shouting my name!

Mathieu Madame Paillardin! (*He moves a pace further in*)

The girls run out of the bathroom and towards the door

Boulot She's called Madame Paillardin.

Marcelle (*moving downstage*) Children. That's all I need. (*She greets them with embarrassment*)

The Girls surround her. Mathieu follows to the L of the group

Boulot moves downstage and stands very close to them, UL of Marcelle

Girls Madame Paillardin! What a lovely surprise! How are you? Madame Paillardin? It's Madame Paillardin.

Boulot (*at her elbow*) Madame Paillardin. Tea is served.

Marcelle Madame Paillardin! He said "Madame Paillardin". He knows my name! (*Worried*) My tea. Oh, thank you. Thank you very much!

Mathieu Your tea? Are you a resident here?

Marcelle No. Not at all! That is to say. . . . Yes! Well it was my husband's idea, as a matter of fact. We're just moving house and so . . .

Mathieu We're in luck's way. We've got the room next door. We shall be neighbours!

Boulot (*loudly*) Madame Paillardin. Your tea is served!

Marcelle (*aside*) He's driving me insane! Is he going to announce my name to the nation?

Boulot (*very loudly*) Madame Paillardin. Your tea . . .

Marcelle Thank you very much.

Boulot moves upstage between the doors

M'sieur. (*She moves to the door of her room*) I'd love to stand here chatting to you.

The others follow her

But my teapot calls. I'm sure you don't want to join me.

Marcelle enters her room, closing the door. She moves to the L end of the fireplace in relief. Mathieu turns to the girls as Marcelle exits, then turns back to her room, opens the door and steps into Marcelle's room. The girls stay in the doorway. Marcelle turns in shock

Mathieu But I'd be delighted! What could be more welcome than a cup of good, hot tea!

Girls Oh yes. Good, hot tea! How lovely! What a treat!

Mathieu (*to Boulot*) Hurry up, my man! Fetch the cups. And look sharp about it.

Boulot As you say, m'sieur.

He exits to room nine

Mathieu (*turning to the girls*) Come along, children. We're all going to pay a call on Madame Paillardin!

Marcelle Help! His jacket. (*She whips Pinglet's hat and jacket from the bed and hides them behind her back*)

Mathieu (*turning his back on Marcelle and moving below the bed*) It's really very pleasant!

Marcelle (*sidling towards the bathroom*) I quite agree. Delightful, isn't it? (*She looks determinedly around the room*)

Eventually Mathieu follows suit and Marcelle throws the hat and jacket into the bathroom and closes the door

Mathieu (*turning to face Marcelle as he hears the door close*) Come along in, children.

The girls move inside the room.

Marcelle My God, how on earth will I get rid of them? (*She forces a smile*)

The girls look around. Pause

Boulot returns downstairs with a tray

Marcelle Very well, then. Do sit down.

Mathieu We don't want to seem difficult. But isn't there a slight shortage of chairs?

Marcelle (*forcing a laugh*) Shortage of chairs? Oh yes. Very witty! Most amusing ...

Boulot enters the room and puts the tray down on the small table

Boulot The tea cups, m'sieur.

Girls Tea! At last ...

Mathieu Fetch us some chairs, porter. And look lively now!

Boulot Very well, m'sieur.

Boulot exits to room nine for more chairs

Mathieu Run along, children. Help the porter. The furniture here seems notable by its absence.

The girls, with Violette leading, follow Boulot

Marcelle (*aside*) Oh my God! Will they never go? And Pinglet's bound to come back in a minute.

Mathieu If I may. (*He moves to L to the table and fiddles with the pot*) I'll put a little more water in the pot.

Marcelle (*in anguish, aside*) He's going to start cooking now! (*Aloud*) Oh, do as you like ...

Boulot comes out of room nine with one chair, moves downstairs, picks up a chair in the hall and re-enters the bedroom. He sets the two chairs at the R *end of the room. Meanwhile, the girls, smallest first, follow him out of room nine, each carrying a chair, re-enter the bedroom and set the chairs in a horizontal line. Violette leaves a space between the second and third chair*

Boulot The chairs, m'sieur.
Marcelle (*aside*) Pinglet! Look what you've landed me in!

As the last chair is being put down, Mathieu moves R *behind them and Boulot moves* L *towards the door. All sit except Marcelle and Boulot*

Boulot I'm going for the bottle.
Marcelle What bottle?
Boulot The hot water bottle. For m'sieur—who is ill.
Mathieu For m'sieur? Who is ill?
Boulot That's just what I said.
Marcelle Get out. Now. Please!

Boulot exits, closing the door. He then exits UR

Thank you. (*Aside*) This charming family's going to kill me! (*She turns to face them*) Please. Do all sit down ...
Mathieu (*sitting judicially on his chair*) We are sitting down.

Marcelle sits with an embarrassed laugh

Apart from that, Madame Paillardin. Is there something troubling you?
Marcelle (*nervously*) Troubling me? Of course not. I feel totally relaxed.
Mathieu Come along, children. Make yourselves useful! Pour out the tea.

Violette rises, moves to the table, pours the cups of tea and passes them along the line

What about your old friend Pinglet, madame? Do you ever see anything of him, these days?
Marcelle Oh, hardly ever! You know how it is in Paris. We've quite lost touch. Of course, I'm a great friend of dear Madame Pinglet. That's why I was there today ...

Pinglet enters UL *and moves to the landing, extremely cheerful*

Pinglet Oh, I'm feeling so much better. I've had a breath of fresh air and I've said "goodbye" to my dinner. I'm fit as a fiddle! And ready for anything! (*He sings whilst moving downstairs*)
Take me where the ladies dance all night.
Take me where the bubbly makes you tight!
Take me where the kisses feel just right ...
In Monte Carlo!

Mathieu's next line overlaps with the last line of the song

Mathieu So you've lost touch with Pinglet?

Marcelle (*wincing as she hears him singing*) Oh, completely. Absolutely lost touch.

Pinglet bounds into the room. All the Mathieu family stand up, astonished

Mathieu ⎫ (*together, in astonishment*) ⎧ Pinglet!
Pinglet ⎭   ⎩ Aaah! The Mathieus!

Marcelle We've had it!

Pinglet (*aside*) Where did they spring from?

Mathieu (*grasping Pinglet's hand*) Pinglet! (*He rises and shakes Pinglet by the hand*)

The girls also rise and stand in front of their chairs. Pervenchie puts her cup back on the tray

My dear old friend! Your ears must be burning. We were just talking about you!

Girls Yes, yes. We were just talking about you. Your ears must be burning.

Pinglet (*moving* DR *to Marcelle and pushing Pervenchie out of the way*) How kind of you. Well, how do you do, Mme Paillardin! How are you! I had some business in the area—I was just passing—and I said to myself, "I'll go and say hello to Mme Paillardin." (*He sits on the second chair from the* R)

The girls sit

Marcelle What a sweet thought. How kind of you. (*She sits*)

Pinglet stands

Girls Yes, yes. What a sweet thought. How kind of you.

Mathieu But do tell me, Pinglet. Do you usually go out in your shirt sleeves?

Pinglet Oh. No. Never. Er. Well, you see. My jacket was torn. So I took it to the tailor. Just in the next street, as a matter of fact. And he said he'd do it in a quarter of an hour, so I said to myself, "Hello," I said, "I've just time to pop in and say hello to Mme Paillardin." (*He sits*)

Marcelle So kind of you. So very kind.

Girls So very kind.

Awkward pause

Pinglet So ... hello!

Marcelle Hello!

Mathieu Hello!

Violette (*moving to the teapot and pouring a cup*) A lovely cup of hot tea. M'sieur Pinglet (*She hands him the cup*)

Pervenchie rises, moves upstage of the chairs to the table and picks up the sugar bowl

Pinglet Tea. How thoughtful of you!

Pervenchie (*moving to Pinglet and crouching on his* L) Sugar, M'sieur Pinglet?

Pinglet (*taking some sugar*) How very kind. (*Aside*) My God ... I didn't exactly come here to have tea with the Mathieu family! (*He shovels endless lumps of sugar in his cup*)

Marguerite You've got a sweet tooth, M'sieur Pinglet.
Pinglet Not at all. Can't stand sugar.

Pervenchie returns the sugar to the tray and returns to sit on the floor

Long pause

Pinglet takes a sip. They all follow his lead. He tries to spit it out but is observed. He manages to swallow it and makes a face. In horror, he sees the others taking another sip. He mimes drinking

Mathieu (*drinking his tea*) Tell me, my dear old friend. What's the news in Paris?
Pinglet The news? Well, we got rid of Marie Antoinette.

Pinglet gives his cup to Pervenchie, who replaces it on the tray, then sits down

Some time ago, of course.
Mathieu And your wife? She's still keeping well? Since this afternoon?
Pinglet Quite well. Thank you. How about yours?
Mathieu (*hurt*) You know perfectly well! She died eight years ago.
Pinglet So she did! I shan't bother to ask after her then. I shan't. Why won't they go?

Boulot enters UR *with a hot-water bottle. He moves into the bedroom, leaving the door open*

Boulot Ah, there you are, m'sieur. Here's m'sieur's hot water bottle.
Marcelle (*aside*) That's all we need!
Pinglet (*aside; taking the hot water bottle*) The tactless idiot! (*He burns his hand on the bottle*) Ouch!
Mathieu What've you got there, Pinglet? Ginger beer?
Pinglet Yes. No! Hot hands. Every time I pass this hotel I order a hot-water bottle.
Mathieu Really?
Pinglet Oh, yes. They're famous here for their good old-fashioned hot-water bottles. Hot water bottles are the spécialité de la maison! My wife, my dear heart Angelique, always says, "If you're passing the Free Trade Hotel, do bring me back one of their glorious old hot-water bottles." Isn't that right, Madame Paillardin?
Marcelle Yes, of course. Quite right. Splendid water bottles! (*In embarrassment*) They're quite the thing here. In Paris.
Boulot But, m'sieur ...
Pinglet That's quite enough! We don't want to hear any more from you, lackey, go along now. Leave the room!
Boulot (*moving to the door*) Very well, m'sieur.

Boulot walks out of the bedroom, up the stairs and exits UL

Pinglet (*closing the door, then to Marcelle*) Madame, I'm sure you must be tired. (*He shouts in Mathieu's* L *ear*) She must be tired ! (*To Marcelle*) I'm not going to keep you up a moment longer. Allow me to take leave of you. (*He opens the door*) I'm going now. No! Don't try and stop me. Goodbye!

Marcelle (*yawning*) Well as a matter of fact . . . (*she rises and gives her cup to Violette*)

Mathieu (*rising*) You're tired? (*He puts his cup on the tray*) But you should have told us. Come along, children.

Pervenche puts her cup on the tray and rises. She takes Paquerette's chair and exits to room nine. The others follow suit in ascending order, each taking the chair to the R *of the one they were sitting on*

Back to our room. Show a little tact and discretion. (*He still has hold of his own chair and begins to follow his daughters*)

Pinglet (*taking hold of Marcelle's chair, then, to Marcelle*) I knew how to flush him out!

Mathieu (*moving to the* R *of Pinglet and putting his chair down, whereupon it gets entangled with Pinglet's*) Good-night, dear Madame Paillardin. You must go straight to bed now.

Pinglet Of course she must!

Pinglet and Mathieu move to pick up their chairs and find they are inextricably entwined

Pinglet (*aside to Marcelle*) I'll go down to put him off the scent. Back in a minute! Stay exactly where you are!

Mathieu backs out of the room with his chair. Pinglet is forced to go too

Marcelle (*closing the door*) This is a pretty kettle of fish!

Mathieu (*holding out his hand to Pinglet*) Good-night my dear old friend. My respects to dear Madame Pinglet!

Pinglet (*putting his chair upside down into Mathieu's hand*) So kind! So very kind!

Pinglet exits quickly UR

Mathieu Goodnight. (*He moves* UC *and puts the two chairs under the hall window*) Come along then children.

The girls move past him into their bedroom and sit on the beds. Mathieu moves to the desk, picks up the candle and goes into the bedroom, closing the door

Marcelle That's enough! That's quite enough! No more adventures! I've learned my lesson . . .

Girls (*moving* C *to kiss Mathieu*) Sleep well, Papa!

Violette We're going to get undressed.

Marcelle puts her bag on the bed

Mathieu Oh, very well. There are your . . . facilities. (*He points to their bathroom*) But quietly now! Madame Paillardin wants to sleep.

The girls exit, into their bathroom, taking their bags and umbrellas. Violette takes the candle

Marcelle I'm not staying a minute longer in this horrible hotel! As soon as Pinglet gets back . . . (*She puts on her coat*)

Mathieu (*yawning*) I'm longing for my bed. (*He picks up his belongings on the bed*)

Marcelle (*searching her room*) My hat! (*She takes the candle and looks under the bed*)

What an evening! Now my hat's done the vanishing trick!

At the same time, Mathieu exits into the UL *bathroom, leaves his belongings there and re-emerges*

Mathieu It's been a long day.

Marcelle Did I put it with Pinglet's bits and pieces?

She takes the candle into the bathroom, leaving the room in darkness

Mathieu (*putting the candle on top of the cigar box on the* C *table*) I think we'll do pretty well here. This room has a sort of rustic simplicity which I find rather appealing. (*He sees Paillardin's belongings*) Good gracious! We've got the luxury of a full toilet set. Tortoise-shell combs! Ebony backed brushes. All the comforts of home. (*He brushes his hair*) Paris hotels are miles ahead of anything we've got in Dieppe. Now, a cigar before turning in! (*He takes out a very small cigar*) There's not much of it, but it's quite enjoyable, such as it is. (*He sees Paillardin's cigar box; to the audience*) A cigar box! "Regalias", hand rolled on the thighs of Cuban beauties. At least eighty centimes a piece. Save this one for a rainy day. (*He puts his own cigar away and lights one from the box*) An A1 hotel de luxe! Seven francs a day and a box of cigars thrown in! (*He takes all the cigars and puts them in his pocket, leaving the cigar box open*) No wonder Pinglet recommended it!

Marcelle emerges from the bathroom

Marcelle (*moving to the* C *of her room*) Incredible! My hat's disappeared. (*She looks in the fireplace*)

Mathieu (*smoking*) An excellent smoke. I can't think how they make a profit!

Marcelle (*putting the candle on the mantelpiece*) And Pinglet's vanished again. Where on earth's he got to?

Mathieu (*moving to the bed* UC *and picking up a nightshirt*) And a nightshirt. Silk from Sulkas. (*He looks in the bag under the bed*) And bedroom slippers. They really think of everything. (*He sits on the bed and picks up the slippers*) What service!

Marcelle moves to her bedroom door and opens it, looking outside

Never known anything like it.

Pinglet enters UR *and moves downstairs to the hall, carrying his hot water bottle*

Marcelle There you are at last!

Pinglet startled, leans against the L *doorway to catch his breath*

Pinglet Here I am at last.

Mathieu (*rising to get his candle and moving to the door*) There's only one thing missing. A nice comforting hot-water bottle! I'll get the porter to bring one.

Marcelle (*to Pinglet*) Come in. Don't hang about!

Mathieu goes out onto the landing with his candle in his hand. It's dark on his R

(*Seeing him*) Drat that man! (*She bangs the door shut and leans against it, listening*)

Pinglet (*aside*) Mathieu! (*He is rooted to the spot*)

Mathieu Goodness me! It's you, Pinglet!

Pinglet (*in embarrassment*) Oh yes. It's me, Pinglet. I had to come back up because there's something I simply had to tell you.

Mathieu Oh? What? (*He puts his candle down on the porter's desk*)

Pinglet (*babbling*) Not that it's all that important. But I might as well tell you. As I'm here . . .

Mathieu Which you obviously are.

Pinglet Yes, well, I think you ought to know this. I was downstairs and I heard people talking. Apparently things were hotting up in Parliament this afternoon.

Mathieu (*uninterested*) Oh, really?

Marcelle sits wearily on the bed

Pinglet Oh yes! There were questions asked about the Budget! I mean, this may astonish you. The Budget came up for discussion! And the Minister of Finance has really been caught with his trousers down. Figuratively, of course!

Mathieu (*bored*) Of course.

Pinglet Well. Where's it going to end? That's what I ask myself. My God, where will it end? And I said there's only one person who knows the answer to that sort of question. Good old Mathieu! So I came straight up here to ask your advice.

Mathieu On the Budget! What on earth do you expect me to do about it?

Pinglet (*cheerfully*) All right then! The Budget bores you. Understood! We'll say no more about the Budget. Good-night to you. I'm on my way . . . (*He starts to leave*)

Mathieu Good-night. But thanks for thinking of me . . . (*He leans on the wall*)

Pinglet Don't mention it. Back to your room now. High time you were in bed, old fellow.

Mathieu I'm waiting for the porter to bring me a hot-water bottle. You told me they were particularly good here.

Pinglet A hot-water bottle! Oh, for God's sake have mine. (*He gives it to him*)

Mathieu I wouldn't dream of it. Robbing you . . . (*He tries to give it back*)

Pinglet You're not robbing me. (*Aside*) It's stone cold anyway. (*Aloud*) I'll pick another up on my way out.

Mathieu It's terribly kind of you. (*He feels the bottle is cold*)

Pinglet Not at all. Think nothing of it. Now then, for God's sake. Get into bed! You must be exhausted.

Mathieu (*standing calmly in his doorway, smoking his cigar*) I certainly am. Good-night to you, Pinglet my dear old fellow.

Pinglet (*waiting for him to go into his room*) Good-night to you! Good-night!

Mathieu (*waving him goodbye*) Good-night!

Pinglet Good-night! What are you waiting for?

Mathieu Oh. Nothing.

Pinglet Good-night to you.

Pinglet exits UR

Mathieu moves into his bedroom, closing the door

Mathieu Charming chap! Forgot my candle!

Pinglet comes back

Mathieu goes back to the landing and finds himself face to face with Pinglet. He smiles at him

Still there, old fellow?

Pinglet (*embarrassed*) I forgot to shake hands.

Pinglet grasps Mathieu's hand, then exits UR

Mathieu returns to his room with the candle

Marcelle rises and wanders around her room

Mathieu (*putting the hot-water bottle on his bed*) Time to get undressed.

Mathieu exits to his bathroom with the candle, nightshirt, slippers and case, leaving his room in darkness

Pinglet re-enters, darting into Marcelle's room

Pinglet (*in Marcelle's room*) I managed it!

Marcelle At last! I thought you'd never get back.

Pinglet But my dearest one. I had to shake off that abominable Mathieu. What a limpet that fellow is!

Marcelle Limpet? The man's a leech!

Pinglet There must be at least a thousand hotels in Paris and he has to pick on this one! Just my luck!

Marcelle Exactly! Well, put on your hat and jacket and let's go home. Please!

Pinglet My hat? My jacket? Where are they?

Marcelle In the bathroom.

Pinglet Oh, thanks.

He exits into the bathroom

Marcelle Oh, and whatever have you done with my hat?

Pinglet re-emerges, putitng on his hat and jacket.

Pinglet Your hat? What about your hat? It must be somewhere.

Marcelle Somewhere? Where? Will you kindly tell me that!

Pinglet (*agitatedly*) Where? Well, I really don't know. When you took it off you put it on the bed. (*He moves to the downstage corner of the bed*) Oh, now I remember. When I was suffocating I used it to fan myself a little. (*He takes his hat off and uses it as a fan*) And then I must have just popped up to the balcony with it in my hand. I suppose I left it upstairs! (*He laughs foolishly*) What a silly billy I am!

Marcelle (*angrily*) I suppose you think that's very funny. Really, Pinglet. You're a genius.

Bastien enters and moves down the stairs

Why on earth did you take it in the first place? Oh, go and get it then. I'll wait for you.

Pinglet Yes. Wait for me! Only wait for me, Marcelle.

Marcelle Well, hurry up. I'm at the end of my tether!

Pinglet rushes into the hall and bumps into Bastien

Pinglet Oh!

Bastien Can I help you, m'sieur?

Pinglet rushes up the stairs

Pinglet I don't need your help! No, thank you. I know where I'm going.

He enters room nine by mistake and comes out again

I know exactly where I'm going.

He exits UL

Bastien Just as well.

Marcelle (*nervously*) It's the last straw! I'm worn out. From now on ... total fidelity!

She goes into her bathroom and closes the door

Bastien is about to sit at the desk when the bell rings

Bastien Good. Good. More guests!

Paillardin enters UR *and moves to the* R *of Bastien*

Ah. It's the m'sieur the learned expert back. (*He lights a candle*)

Paillardin In person!

Bastien M'sieur the learned expert is going to bed?

Paillardin If that is quite convenient to you. You have my candle?

Bastien Here it is, m'sieur the learned expert.

Paillardin (*smiling*) And have your worthy ghosts made their appearance yet?

Bastien Not so far as I am aware, m'sieur the learned expert. (*He gives Paillardin the candle*)

Paillardin Perhaps they were caught in the traffic.

He goes into the room on the L *and moves to the* C, *leaving the door open*

Bastien Laugh while you can, m'sieur the learned expert. Laugh while you can!

He follows Paillardin and stands in the doorway

Paillardin (*laughing and looking round the room*) The haunted chamber doesn't look particularly haunted to me. I just hope your ghosts have the good manners to let a fellow get a decent bit of shut-eye.
Bastien They probably heard you say that, m'sieur the learned expert.
Paillardin (*moving to the* C *table and seeing his open cigar box*) Some joker's been at my cigars! (*He puts the candle on the table*)
Bastien M'sieur the learned expert?
Paillardin (*showing Bastien the empty box*) I told you. My cigars. The box was full when I went out. Who's been at my cigars, eh?
Bastien I have absolutely no idea, m'sieur.
Paillardin You have absolutely no idea! Well, my cigars didn't suddenly decide to go out for a breath of fresh air.
Bastien (*gloomily*) It's obvious, isn't it.
Paillardin What's obvious?
Bastien It's the supernatural. Up to their usual tricks m'sieur!
Paillardin Don't make me laugh. Whoever saw a ghost smoking a Havana cigar?
Bastien I don't see why not. You do it.
Paillardin Look at this. My brushes. My comb! All at sixes and sevens. The ghosts have been brushing their hair.
Bastien Seems the most likely explanation.
Paillardin I think I'm beginning to get to the bottom of this little mystery. (*He moves to Bastien*) There's some thieving rascal who pays calls here pretending to be a ghost.
Bastien Oh ye of little faith! (*He crosses himself*)
Paillardin All right. Run along now, my man I'll have it out tomorrow— with your superior. (*He returns to the* C *of the room*)
Bastien As you say, m'sieur. I hope you sleep as well as possible.

He exits from the room and closes the door

Under the circumstances. (*Aside*) And I hope some bloody great ghost comes and gives you a slosh around the chops, m'sieur the learned expert.

He exits UR

Paillardin Oh yes! There's a thief at work here. That's perfectly obvious. (*He looks at his brush*) He's even left his filthy thieving hairs in my brushes. (*He puts his brushes and combs back in his bag*)

Pinglet enters UL, *carrying his hat. He next speaks from downstage of the upper landing*

Paillardin picks up his candle and moves UC *to the bed*

Pinglet Nothing! Not a sign of her wretched hat. And I've searched high and low. (*He continues walking down the stairs*)

Paillardin (*looking at the bed*) My night shirt and bedroom slippers! The fellow's a nightwear robber and he's made a killing! (*He hangs up his hat, puts his candle down and takes out a book*)

Pinglet Marcelle's going to cut up pretty rough about her hat! Never mind. I'll just have to tell her the truth. Courage, Pinglet!

He enters Marcelle's room

Paillardin I'll just have to sleep in my clothes. At least if anything supernatural crops up I'll be ready for action. (*He lies on the bed and starts to read a book*)

Marcelle returns from the bathroom and moves to the mantelpiece

Marcelle Back at last! Give me my hat and let's go.
Pinglet Marcelle. I want you to be very brave about this.
Marcelle Why've I got to be brave? Tell me, Pinglet. Why?
Pinglet I have not recovered your hat. Some swine's pinched it!
Marcelle Who?
Pinglet He didn't leave his card.
Marcelle Charming! Never mind. Luckily I brought my little mantilla. (*She puts on a lace mantilla from her bag*)

Pinglet picks up the bag and opens the door

Well, what are we waiting for?
Pinglet Very well! The order for retreat.

Pinglet exits into the hall and moves UR

Marcelle What an evening! It's taught me a lesson . . . (*She follows Pinglet*) What a lesson!

Pinglet and Marcelle exit UR

Paillardin (*yawning*) I'm absolutely whacked. Can't think what's the matter with me. Can't keep my eyes open. (*He puts out his candle and draws the bed curtains*)

Pinglet and Marcelle rush back into the hall

Marcelle Oh, my God! It's Maxime! (*She rushes past Pinglet towards the* R *bedroom*)
Pinglet Your husband's nephew here with Victoire, my maid! The younger generation's got absolutely no sense of morality!
Marcelle Get in there.

Marcelle pulls Pinglet into the bedroom and closes the door

Marcelle Lock the door!
Pinglet (*in a panic angrily*) But the key! Where on earth's the key? What happened to the key?
Marcelle Lock the door! Never mind the key!

Pinglet I can't lock it! Not without the key. (*He jumps up and down, then points to the bathroom*) In there! (*He rushes towards the bathroom*)
Marcelle Is there a key?
Pinglet There's a bolt on the door. Quick!

He exits into the bathroom

Marcelle What a night! My God! What a nightmare!

She follows Pinglet into the bathroom

Victoire and Maxime enter UR *and move to the hall. Maxime has a book. He takes his hat off as he enters and holds it in his* L *hand. Victoire carries an umbrella. Bastien enters with them*

Bastien This way, m'sieur. Welcome to the Free Trade Hotel.
Maxime (*to Victoire*) This is a serious step we're taking, mademoiselle . . .
Victoire Oh, don't keep on about how serious it is.
Bastien (*in honeyed tones*) Now, may I say that I know exactly what m'sieur and madame are looking for! A charming little love nest where you and madame can snuggle down and no questions asked! M'sieur is clearly a man of taste and discernment.
Maxime (*very worried*) Oh . . . yes. Do you really think so?
Bastien (*moving to the desk and lighting a candle*) By a happy chance I am able to offer m'sieur and madame room number nine. It was in that very room that the Crown Princess of Poland spent her wedding night, with her majordomo. You'll be thoroughly at home there, madame!
Victoire In a princess's room!
Bastien In this hotel, madame, you bed down with the élite!
Victoire Oh, I know. We've read your brochure. That's it then. We'll take number nine.
Bastien That's wonderful. (*He starts to laugh*) You'll have the time of your young lives in number nine. (*He laughs whilst looking at them*)

Bastien goes upstairs with a candle and the drill

Maxime (*to Victoire*) He's laughing at me! Even the porter's laughing at me!
Victoire Don't worry. Let him laugh!

Victoire pulls Maxime upstairs

Bastien (*on the landing*) If madame and m'sieur would condescend to enter. . . . (*He gestures to room nine*)

Bastien enters room nine

Maxime (*holding back*) Mademoiselle. Careful. Please. I really don't know where all this is going to end . . .
Victoire Why not come in and find out?
Maxime I'm all prepared, anyway. Thank God I've revised my Descartes.

Victoire pulls Maxime into room nine. He gives a yell

The girls enter from their bathroom, wearing their nightdresses. They close the door and move C. *Violette puts the candle on the* C *table and moves* UR *to her bed*

Violette (*putting down her candle*) Early to bed! (*She sits down on the* R)
Marguerite That's going to be my bed! (*She moves to the* DL *bed and jumps onto it*)
Pervenchie I want that one. It looks lovely and big. (*She also jumps onto it, pushing Marguerite*)
Paquerette No. I bag that one! (*She gets onto the same bed*)
Pervenchie I bagged it before you bagged it!
Paquerette You're a liar. I saw it hours ago.
Pervenchie You saw it but you never bagged it, did you?
Paquerette Anyway, you smell!

An argument starts

Violette (*rushing to the others and whispering*) Don't make such an unholy row, girls! Papa told us not to.

They all sit on their own beds

How lovely it's going to be ... to slip between the sheets. (*She gets into bed*) Crikey! It's freezing!
Marguerite Let's have your candle. (*She moves to the candle on the table*)
Pervenchie No, it's mine!
Paquerette Mine.
Pervenchie You thief.

They quarrel over the candle, which drops onto the floor

Violette That's our candle gone!
Pervenchie Butter fingers!

Bastien enters from room nine and moves downstage

Bastien Sweet dreams, m'sieur! Sleep well, madame!

Bastien moves downstairs and exits through the door UR

Violette fetches four nightlights from the L *bathroom*
The other girls crowd around her as she lights them, then each girl picks up a light and carries it to her bed. Each girl then climbs, in turn, on her own bed to say her line

Violette What lovely night lights! Do we look like little elves ...?
Pervenchie Or terrible ghosts!
Violette That's what we are! I'm the headless hunter of Honfleur!
Paquerette I'm the strangled Sister of Soissons!
Marguerite I'm the noseless Nun of Nantes!

They are all standing up on their beds. Paquerette starts to sing

Paquerette (*singing*)
                    Knock! Knock! Knock!
                    Wake up ghosts. All come out of your graves!

Girls (*singing and making ghostly movements*)
>>> Wake up ghosts, we're going to dance
>>> Up and down the roads of France.
>>> Rattling bones till break of day
>>> The Headless Hunter leads the way!
>>> Knock, knock, knock,
>>> Wake up ghosts, come out of your graves!

Paillardin (*waking up, terrified, his head appearing between the curtains*) The ghosts are here! Oh my God!

The girls dance clockwise round the room and over the beds (missing out the UL bed). They sing in canon

Girls   Wake up ghosts, we're going to dance.
>>> Up and down the roads of France!
>>> Rattling bones till break of day.
>>> The headless dancer leads the way!

Paillardin throws the curtains aside and holds his brushes up as a crucifix. The girls have now completed one circuit of the room

Paillardin Evil spirits, avaunt!
Girls Aah! It's a man! Ooh! Help!

They shriek and rush into the bathroom UL

Paillardin flings the brushes away in fright. He is rooted to the spot—still standing on his bed

Paillardin The ghosts! The knocking ghosts! Help! Help!

Victoire rushes onto the landing minus her hat, umbrella and jacket. Her blouse is undone

Victoire rushes down the stairs as Paillardin runs out of his room

Victoire What's going on?
Paillardin (*shouting*) Help me! Help me!
Victoire (*face to face with Paillardin*) Monsieur Paillardin!

Maxime follows Victoire out of room nine and sees Paillardin as he reaches the window area of the hall

Maxime My uncle!

He rushes back upstairs and into room nine

Paillardin follows him in panic towards the exit UL

Victoire breaks DR of Paillardin as she recognizes him and rushes into the L bedroom. She jumps on to the UC bed and draws the curtains, leaving a slight gap on the onstage side

Paillardin The ghosts have arrived! The knocking ghosts! Get thee behind me Satan! Beelzebub!

Paillardin exits UL

Mathieu comes out of his bathroom with a candle and moves to the UC *bed*

Mathieu What's all this fuss about? A man in here? Where on earth's the man? In the bed? I don't see any man. (*He pulls the curtain back and sees Victoire*)

Victoire Oh!

Mathieu Excuse me, madame! (*He laughs*) They told me you were a man. (*He draws the curtains*) You're quite clearly not a man at all!

He returns to the bathroom with his candle

(*Speaking as he goes*) What on earth was all that fuss about? It's not a man at all. It's a woman!

The bedroom is now in darkness

Girls (*off*) No . . . no, Papa. It really is a man.

Maxime enters from room nine, carrying his and Victoire's belongings

Maxime My uncle's cleared off. I'd better rescue Victoire. (*He moves downstairs to the hall*) No one about! (*He whispers*) Victoire!

Maxime goes into the L *bedroom*

Victoire (*peeping out of the curtains*) Here I am!

The UL *bathroom door opens. Victoire grabs Maxime and pulls him into bed and closes the curtains*

Mathieu comes out of the bathroom, followed by the girls, and moves DL *of the bed*

Maxime and Victoire put their jackets on behind the curtains

Mathieu Here you are, my children. See for yourselves!

Maxime and Victoire give small cries and try to hide

Violette My dear Papa. I can assure you. It's a man. We saw him. Large as life!

Mathieu And I've got eyes as well. What're you suggesting? That I've reached my time of life and I still can't tell a man from a woman? Let me tell you, I have memories!

Mathieu turns to the bed as Victoire slips out and exits into the hall. The girls do not see her

There you are, you see. I know what I'm talking about. It's a perfectly obvious woman!

Mathieu turns to face the girls as Maxime also slips out. The girls see him

Girls No, no, Papa! Look. Look closely! Can't you see? It's a man!

Mathieu (*turning and seeing Maxime in the doorway briefly, then facing the audience*) Could it be both?

Maxime (*grabbing Victoire by the hand*) Let's go.

Victoire Yes. Let's!

They exit UR

Mathieu We've got to get to the bottom of this!

Mathieu puts his candle down on the C *table and moves into the hall. The girls follow*

Porter! Porter!

Boulot enters UL *and comes down the stairs*

Boulot What's all this noise about? (*He moves to Mathieu*)
Mathieu Oh, porter. What on earth's going on? There are men and women, of both sorts, in our room!
Boulot Really, m'sieur? Then undoubtedly m'sieur has seen "them".
Mathieu Them! Who are "them"?
Boulot Them. Who are "them" indeed. Them whose names we dare not speak, m'sieur. But you were in the haunted room.
All The haunted room!

The girls back towards their father. Mathieu turns and looks at the haunted room

Paillardin enters and tiptoes down the stairs, reaching the fourth step during Boulot's speech

Boulot Oh yes, m'sieur! Those men and women you were talking about. They're not men and women of this world, m'sieur. They are the departed! But they do not rest in peace, m'sieur. They come back here to haunt our visitors. We call them "the knocking ghosts".
Girls (*with little cries of terror*) The knocking ghosts! Poor, troubled spirits! Aaaaah!

The girls scream and run upstairs

Paillardin screams and runs up in front of them. They all exit UL

Mathieu (*following his girls*) Children! I don't know what's got into you. Running round the hotel in your nightgowns! What would they say at the convent? Children! Children!

Mathieu exits UL

Boulot (*moving downstage and speaking at the same time as Mathieu*) A curse is on our house! A terrible curse!

Boulot exits UL

Meanwhile Pinglet comes out of his bathroom, followed by Marcelle, who closes the bathroom door

Pinglet What's all the hullabaloo? Are we on fire? (*He moves to the* C *of the room*)
Marcelle Whatever it is, it's nothing ordinary. Let's get out of this place before I die of terror.
Pinglet Yes, but careful! Don't take any risks. (*He opens the door a crack*)

Marcelle Oh, the joy of not being in this ghastly hotel!
Pinglet (*looking round the landing*) The coast's clear!

Marcelle steps into the hall, followed by Pinglet

Marcelle (*with a sigh of relief*) Safe at last! (*She moves towards the* UR *exit*)

Paillardin comes rushing madly down the stairs

Paillardin The ghosts are back! The knocking ghosts!
Marcelle (*terrified*) Oh, my God! Get back in!

Marcelle rushes back into the bedroom. Pinglet is still in the doorway

Paillardin Thank God! Living beings!

Pinglet rushes into the bedroom, holding the door open while asking the question

Pinglet Who is it?
Marcelle Oh. Nobody. Only my husband!
Pinglet (*terrified*) Help! (*He shuts the door in Paillardin's face and pushes against it*)
Paillardin (*who has seen them without recognizing them*) Open up there! Let me in! (*He tries to open the door*) For mercy's sake!
Pinglet (*holding the door*) This is private property. No entry! Absolutely no entry!
Paillardin (*still pulling the door*) Please!

He manages to open the door a little but Pinglet forces it shut

   I beg of you. I'm in terrible danger from ghosts! For God's sake let me in!
Pinglet No entry!

Paillardin again gets the door open a little and Pinglet forces it shut

Marcelle Don't let him in!
Pinglet No entry! I may not have much choice. He's stronger than I am.

Paillardin forces the door open and charges in, leaving the door open

   Pinglet dives into the fireplace as Marcelle grabs Paillardin's hat and pulls it right down over her head, hiding her face

Paillardin My hat's gone! Excuse me, madame, that's my hat you're wearing! (*He tries to take it back*)
Marcelle (*hanging onto the hat*) Help me! Help me!

Pinglet extricates himself from the fireplace. His face is covered with soot. He taps Paillardin on the back

Paillardin (*turning*) Aaah! The chimney sweep?

Marcelle breaks downstage and slips onto her knees

Pinglet punches Paillardin around the room then gives him a kick in the back which sends him through the open door into the hall

(*Moving downstage*) It's another ghost! A knocking ghost! They're in a terrible mood tonight!

Paillardin exits UR

Pinglet closes the door and turns to face Marcelle, hat in hand, leaning on the door in relief

Pinglet Well. I think that's seen him off the premises.
Marcelle (*taking off her hat and putting it on the floor*) At last! What a narrow squeak! (*She turns to face Pinglet*) My God! A blackamoor!
Pinglet No! No it's me. Pinglet.
Marcelle (*weakly*) This night'll be the death of me. You, Pinglet? You've undergone some sort of colour change . . .
Pinglet What are you talking about?
Marcelle When I think back. Oh what we've lived through! It makes me feel completely dizzy!
Pinglet (*moving to her, whilst putting on his hat*) It's all over now. We can breathe again.
Marcelle What a blessed relief!
Pinglet Isn't it marvellous! Our troubles are over, Marcelle. We're safe at last. (*He gives her his hand and starts to help her up*)

The sound of raised voices and police whistles is heard

What the devil's that? (*He drops her*)
Marcelle (*falling onto the floor*) Not something new?

Bastien enters UR *and moves to the* C. *He calls in at the* L *door then opens the* R *door and calls in, leaving the door open*

Bastien Oh, my God! It's the police! The police!
Pinglet (*to Marcelle*) Hide! (*He throws the rug over her, then tries to get under the bed but is unable to*)
Bastien Make yourselves scarce, messieurs and mesdames! It's the Department of Public Morality. (*He moves upstairs to the landing*) The Morals are coming! Aaaah!

Bastien turns at the landing, sees the police enter UR, *gives a scream and a little jump and exits* UL, *shouting as he goes*

The Morals are coming!

The police see Bastien and give chase, blowing their whistles and shouting "there he is!"

Marcelle (*to Pinglet*) What's he talking about!
Pinglet (*jumping up and down in terror*) The Morals. The Department of Public Morality. That is to say, the police!

Marcelle gets up

We're absolutely and completely in the soup!
Marcelle The police! No! That's the last straw! I'm leaving now. (*She rushes into the hall*)

Boucard, carrying an umbrella, enters UR. *He is followed by two constables*

Pinglet follows Marcelle out of the bedroom

My God! An inspector!

Marcelle rushes back into the bedroom and slams the door in Pinglet's face as he turns to follow her

Boucard There goes one of them. (*He points to Pinglet*) Arrest him, lads!

Pinglet tries to run away DC *but the constables give chase and overpower him in one swift move. Pinglet drops on his knees in the struggle*

Pinglet I can assure you, m'sieur. There's a perfectly innocent explanation!

The police force his head down

Constable Tell us down at the station.
Boucard (*tapping on the* R *door with his umbrella*) There's a woman in there!

The constable forces the door half open

Marcelle No entry! Absolutely no entry! (*She succeeds in closing the door*)
Boucard (*to the constables*) Force it!

The constable forces the door with his shoulder. It flies open. Marcelle recoils to the fireplace

Marcelle I'm lost!
Boucard Bring her out here! (*He moves downstage*)
Constable Come along with me, madame.

He ushers Marcelle into the hall

Marcelle I can't believe it!
Pinglet The poor woman!
Marcelle It's all a terrible mistake, m'sieur. I'm a completely honest woman!
Pinglet She's perfectly right. She's a completely honest woman.
Boucard So much the better. (*To Pinglet*) No one asked your opinion! Constable. Take the gentleman through there! (*He points to the room on the* L)
Pinglet (*resisting*) Now look here, my man!
Constable Come along now. We've heard quite enough from you.

They take him into the room on the L, *one constable standing guard outside the closed door*

Boucard (*to Marcelle*) And as for you, madame. Don't give me any fairy stories. Name and identity, if you please.
Marcelle But, m'sieur. What on earth's this all about? I'm here with my husband.
Boucard (*shrugging*) I did say, no fairy stories.
Marcelle But it's perfectly true! I'm the wife of the gentleman. ... The gentleman who has just gone in there with your gentlemen.

Boucard (*smiling at her*) Oh, yes, of course. The lawful wedded wife! Proud possessor of a marriage certificate! I'm quite sure you are. And would it be taking too much of a liberty to enquire madame's name?

Marcelle But, m'sieur ... (*aside*) My God. It's the only way out! (*To Boucard*) Certainly. My name's Madame Pinglet.

Boucard Very well, madame. (*To the constable*) Bring back that individual, constable. (*He points to the* L)

Constable (*opening the door and calling to Pinglet*) All right, you. The Inspector wants you. (*He manhandles Pinglet* DCL)

Pinglet (*crossing the landing, aside*) That poor little helpless woman! She won't have had the presence of mind to give a false name.

The other constable exits from the bedroom and stands outside the R *bedroom door*

Boucard (*to Pinglet*) All right, m'sieur. Full name please. No fairy tales!

Pinglet (*aside*) Got it! It's the only way to save her. Thank God I'm brilliant! (*To Boucard, with great self confidence*) I really can't understand what this is all about. It's perfectly above board. This lady is my wife!

Marcelle (*seeing a ray of hope*) Of course I am.

Boucard (*aside*) Could they be fooling me by telling the truth? (*To Pinglet*) Just your name, m'sieur. If you please.

Pinglet Madame's already told you it, I'm sure. (*Loud and clearly*) I am Monsieur Henry Paillardin!

Marcelle Oh, my God!

Boucard (*politely*) Thank you so very much, m'sieur. It's just exactly as I thought!

Marcelle (*aside*) He's sunk me!

Pinglet (*aside, pleased*) I've saved her!

As the whistle sounds upstairs a whole stream of people emerge at the top of the stairs and run down in panic in the following order—three "lingerie" girls, three men, Boulot, Bastien, Mathieu, his four daughters and three policemen. The constable at the bottom of the stairs rushes to the door UR *to block off their retreat. The action then proceeds as follows in each of the rooms*

R *bedroom*

The 1st man, Moody, tries to get in the door but the 2nd man, Lloyd, tries also, and they become wedged. On freeing himself, Moody teeters DR *taking a candle from the mantlepiece*

Lloyd tries to get under the bed as one of the girls tries to get into the fireplace. Pervenchie gets to the C *of the room as a policeman grabs the girl's leg as she disappears up the chimney*

L *bedroom*

Another "lingerie" girl gets into the UC *bed and draws the curtains as Boucard shouts "stop". She then exits in panic. Boulot moves towards the* UL *bathroom. The 3rd "lingerie" girl moves to the* DR *bed. Bastien moves to the* C *of the room and picks up a candle. Violette gets just inside the door*

Hall

Paquerette gets to the doorway of the R *room. Marguerite moves down-stage. Mathieu moves to the* L *bedroom door. One constable is on the 2nd stair, another at the bottom of the stairs*

Boucard (*shouting as the last of the constables appears*) Stop!

Everyone stops moving. Silence

Take the whole boiling down to the police station!
All To the police station!

Noise and panic start again. They all rush from their rooms, trying to hide or exit as the lights fade

When the stage is in darkness, the sound of a slamming door is heard

Exits

DR *Boucard and two constables, one holding a candle*
CL *Bastien, holding a candle, Pinglet*
UL *Mathieu, Violette, Marguerite*

CURTAIN

ACT III

M. Pinglet's Office. Early the next morning

When the CURTAIN *rises the room is deserted and the window at the far end is open. The clock strikes seven*

On Lights up, Pinglet appears at the window still with a blackened face. He climbs into the room and hauls the ladder up. It takes a long time and he pauses for a look at the audience halfway through. He returns the ladder to the window seat, closes the window and puts his hat back on the L *end of the seat. He then moves downstage and sits briefly on his stool for his first line*

Pinglet My God! What a night! What a ghastly night . . . (*he runs down the stairs and checks the* UR *door*) Still locked. She's not back, thank God. At least Madame Pinglet wasn't there. (*He moves above the chaise, taking his jacket off*) She must have been the only one. And when she gets back . . . she'll find me looking like a man who's just got out of bed.

He exits UL *briefly to exchange his jacket for a dressing gown and re-enters on hearing the sound of footsteps and a knock at the door. He leaves the bedroom door ajar*

Is that you dear heart! It can't be her. Anyway, she's got a key. She never knocks. (*He moves above the chaise*)

Victoire (*off*) It's me, m'sieur. Victoire.

Pinglet The little baggage! She was at the Free Trade Hotel—along with the rest of the world! But I can't tick her off about it without giving myself away. (*He calls*) What do you want?

Victoire Your hot chocolate, m'sieur.

Pinglet Oh, very good. Wheel it in . . .

Victoire (*off*) How can I? The door's locked.

Pinglet (*moving* L *of the* UR *door*) Of course it is! Well, go and ask madame for the key.

Victoire (*off*) But madame's not back yet, m'sieur.

Pinglet Not back! Good heavens. Her sister must have taken a turn for the worse. It must add greatly to the terrors of being ill, having Madame Pinglet looming up at your bedside!

Victoire (*off*) So what does m'sieur want me to do?

Pinglet Drink it yourself. I haven't got the key. You'll have to wait till madame comes back.

Victoire (*off*) Very well, m'sieur.

Pinglet (*moving to the* DR *desk, picking up the key and putting it in his pocket*) Of course I could unlock the door. But if I do . . . Bang goes my alibi! All the same. What a night! What a terrible night! Dragged off to the police station like a couple of pickpockets, and I hardly got time to steal a kiss! (*He sits on the sofa, and puts his feet up*) The Free Trade Hotel! I'd have had a more passionate evening at the Building Contractors' Annual Dinner! Anyway, why should the Department of Morality complain about me and Marcelle? Her husband wasn't complaining.

There is a knock at the door

(*Rising; to himself*) Who's there? Who's there . . .?
Marcelle (*off, in a hushed voice*) Pinglet! It's me.
Pinglet Who's me?
Marcelle (*off*) Me. Marcelle!
Pinglet (*rushing to the door*) At last! Are you alone?
Marcelle (*off*) Of course I am. Open up!
Pinglet Half a minute. (*He unlocks the door*) Now. Pull the bolt on your side.
Pinglet (*letting Marcelle in*) Come on in. Look slippy!

Marcelle enters and rushes straight below the chaise

(*Locking the door*) Oh, Marcelle! What a night! My God, what a night. . . . We've gone through a baptism of fire.
Marcelle (*moving upstage in agitation*) Oh, Pinglet! Pinglet! You've ruined my reputation!
Pinglet (*following to her* R) Don't be ridiculous. I haven't ruined anything. I mean, just because we happen to have been caught in a hotel bedroom together—What's that got to do with it?

Marcelle gives a sob

Anyway, we're not undesirable characters. Police raids are only meant for undesirable characters.
Marcelle Looking at you, Pinglet, I suppose you might be described as extremely undesirable . . . I always thought so.
Pinglet (*kissing Marcelle and transferring a sooty smut to her nose from his*) Darling Marcelle.
Marcelle Better call me Madame Paillardin. In the circumstances.
Pinglet Darling Madame Paillardin.

Marcelle sits on the L *end of the chaise. Pinglet sits on the* R *end*

Your husband need never know!
Marcelle He'll find out somehow. The police'll never leave us alone now. . . . And the newspapers. . . . We're doomed, Pinglet! We're both doomed! (*She collaspses onto the chaise*)
Pinglet Chin up, Madame Paillardin. We've got absolutely nothing to feel guilty about. Worse luck. Try to be brave.
Marcelle All right. (*She pulls herself together*)
Pinglet (*examining her face*) I say, old thing. You've got a smut on your nose.
Marcelle A smut? Me? Well, you must have put it there. (*She rises, moves to the sideboard* UL *and picks up the mirror*)

Pinglet Me?

Marcelle Just look at your face!

Pinglet (*moving to her*) Mine?

Marcelle gives him the mirror. He looks in it, then gives a second look

Pinglet Oh, my God! Soot! From the fireplace. The chimney can't have been swept for years. (*He takes the mirror to the* DL *desk, puts it down and begins cleaning himself with a napkin and water on the tray*) I'd have had a fine chance of convincing Madame Pinglet that I've just got out of my lonely bed. Troubles! Nothing but troubles and tribulations!

Marcelle Oh yes! What tremendous troubles! What terrible tribulations! (*In a matter of fact voice*) After you with the water.

Pinglet hands her the napkin and she removes the smut from her nose. He moves upstage a little for her to get to the mirror

Pinglet But it might have been worse. We might have spent the night in the cells, like the others. But thank God the Inspector trusted us and let us go.

Marcelle Well, of course! That was because he could see the sort of people he was dealing with.

Pinglet (*taking the napkin from Marcelle and continuing to clean himself*) And because I stumped up five thousand francs bail! (*He shows her his face*) All gone now, has it?

Marcelle Just a little speck. On the end of your nose. (*She clutches his arm*) Five thousand francs!

Pinglet I offered him the choice. My word as a gentleman or five thousand francs. He took the money. Oh, and I have to prove our identity to his satisfaction by this afternoon.

Marcelle That's torn it! (*She moves behind the chaise*) You can't possibly prove that you're Monsieur Paillardin! It would have been so easy not to have landed us in all these complications. Why on earth did you have to call yourself Monsieur Paillardin when you're obviously Monsieur Pinglet?

Pinglet (*putting the mirror down*) Well really. Wasn't it just a tiny bit your fault? If only you hadn't said you were Madame Pinglet when everyone knows you're Madame Paillardin!

Marcelle Excuse me! I only called myself Madame Pinglet so they'd think I was your wife!

Pinglet Excuse me! I only called myself Monsieur Paillardin so they'd think I was your husband! (*He moves* UC *and stuffs the dirty napkin into his case on the rostrum*)

Marcelle But use your common sense, my dear Pinglet. If you've got any left! How on earth are you going to convince the Inspector that your wife's called Madame Pinglet when you've made it perfectly clear to him that your name's Paillardin?

Pinglet Let's be perfectly honest about this, old girl. When I said I was Paillardin, how on earth was I to know that you'd gone to the extraordinary lengths of introducing yourself as Madame Pinglet?

Marcelle (*in irritation*) Well, if you didn't know that you should have kept your mouth shut!

Pinglet (*aside*) Women! They've got an answer for everything.

There is a knock at the door

Who's there?

Paillardin (*off*) It's me! Paillardin!

Marcelle (*whispering*) Oh God! My husband ... (*She rushes to the chaise and throws herself flat on it*)

Pinglet Ssh! (*To Paillardin, as he moves to the door*) What do you want, old chap? (*He looks round for Marcelle, wondering where she has gone*)

Paillardin (*off*) I want to speak to you. Open the door!

Pinglet I can't. My wife's locked me in and gone off with the key.

Paillardin (*off*) What a woman!

Pinglet Tell you what. Go outside. Get the gardener's long ladder. And come in by the window!

Paillardin (*off*) I'll go and get the ladder.

Pinglet Good idea!

Sound of departing footsteps

Marcelle (*tiptoeing to Pinglet*) Now! Let me out.

Pinglet (*listening*) Wait! His footsteps are dying away. (*He opens the door*) Out you go! (*He goes to the window to see if he can see Paillardin and comes back*)

Marcelle (*leaning in the doorway*) What a night!

Pinglet (*moving to open the window*) Yes. Indeed yes. My God! What a night! (*He shouts down to Paillaridn*) Are you there, old chap?

Paillardin (*off*) Come up! My dear fellow. Aren't you ashamed to be treated like that—by a woman!

Pinglet Just part of the wear and tear of married life!

Paillardin (*off*) My God. If my wife ever treated me like that!

He appears at the window. Marcelle is out of his sight behind the door

Of course, she wouldn't dare. The poor little thing loves me far too much.

Pinglet (*returning to the door*) Bolt the door after you. (*To Paillardin*) Steady on. Mind how you go. (*He locks the door then turns back towards the window*)

Paillardin climbs in the window. He has a huge black eye

Paillardin Oh, my friend. (*He moves downstage*) What a night I've had, what a night!

Pinglet Is there something the matter with your eye, old chap?

Paillardin (*moving towards Pinglet*) There are more things in heaven and earth, Pinglet, than dreamt of in your philosophies.

Pinglet What sort of things?

Paillardin Supernatural manifestations! (*He moves to the armchair and sits*) Oh, I was like you once. I used to scoff.

Pinglet moves to the DR end of the chaise

No longer! I have seen, Pinglet, what I have seen. And I tell you quite frankly. I never want to see it again.

Pinglet (*sitting on the chaise*) Oh, really? What's that?

Paillardin Ghosts! Troubled spirits of the departed.

Pinglet (*laughing*) Ghosts!

Paillardin Oh yes. I thought I was very clever when I agreed to sleep in that accursed hotel! I put it all down to the central heating. What a fool I was! I tell you. I'd hardly put my head on my pillow in the haunted room when I was wide awake. And I saw them! (*He rises and moves to Pinglet*) Devilish apparitions. (*He screams at Pinglet who retreats* DL. *Paillardin follows*) With unearthly voices. They were dancing, a wild frenzied dance. (*He mimes the ghosts movements, skipping clockwise around the chaise*) A terrible dance. Singing. Singing in a way that was hardly human!

Pinglet laughs

> (*Grabbing Pinglet by his lapels*) Mock on, Pinglet! Mock on. I shall never forget that blood chilling song. (*He sings, moving towards the chaise*) (*Jumping on the chaise*)
> > Wake up you ghosts, we're going to dance
> > Up and down the roads of France.
> > Rattling bones till break of day
> > The headless Hunter's on his way!

It would have frozen your blood!

Pinglet (*aside*) It would have done. If they'd sung like that!

Paillardin It didn't stand on ceremony! I gathered up my bits and pieces ... (*he climbs down and moves to the* R *end of the chaise*) and I was off, like a bat out of hell! Oh, that room ... that damnable hotel bedroom! It was horrible. I fled and saw two normal human beings in another room ...

Pinglet (*moving in a pace, not thinking*) Number ten.

Paillardin Number ten? Why should it have been Number ten?

Pinglet Oh, I don't know. Why shouldn't it have been number ten?

Paillardin All right. Let's say it was number ten. I moved over to it and saw ...

Pinglet (*moving closer to Paillardin*) Yes?

Paillardin A woman!

Pinglet Ah ...

Paillardin Or at least, something that looked like a woman ... something in a dress and with ... (*he gestures, showing breasts, etc*) I couldn't tell if it had a head, because of my hat.

Pinglet It was over your eyes?

Paillardin No.

Pinglet No?

Paillardin No! It was over *its* eyes.

Pinglet Remarkable!

Paillardin The accursed apparition was wearing my hat. But the dress. Oh yes. I'd know that dress anywhere.

Pinglet My God!

Paillardin It was a sickening sort of puce colour. The colour of old blood, Pinglet!

Pinglet (*aside*) Damn!

Paillardin (*grabbing Pinglet's lapels*) But at that very moment! Now this was witchcraft! Devilish withcraft! A ghostly chimney sweep materialized from the fireplace! An evil spirit, of course.

Pinglet Naturally.

Paillardin Supernaturally! A ghostly chimney sweep, about your size. (*He looks away from Pinglet for a moment*)

Pinglet (*positively*) Couldn't have been. Must've been bigger. (*He bends his knees slightly*)

Paillardin What do you mean? Must've been bigger?

Pinglet (*confused*) Chimney sweeps are always bigger. Even after death.

Paillardin You could be right. I hardly had time to measure it. Before I knew where I was it fell on me savagely and gave me a punch in the ...

Pinglet shuffles (with his knees still bent) L to the desk and sits on the chair

... face, and then I got a kick up the ...

Pinglet It was the kick that gave you the black eye?

Paillardin No. It was the punch. Never again. I tell you. I'll never set foot in that hotel again! Oh, my dear old friend. God preserve you from the knocking ghosts! (*He staggers back and sits on the chaise*)

Pinglet And does your lady wife believe these tales of the supernatural?

Paillardin My wife! I haven't seen her yet. When I got home I knocked and knocked at her bedroom door. No answer!

Pinglet (*aside*) We're lost!

Paillardin She was sleeping like a log. I had to spend the rest of the night in my dressing-room.

Maxime (*off*) Uncle! Are you there, uncle?

Paillardin That sounds like young Maxime! (*He moves quickly to the window*)

Pinglet (*following him to the bottom of the stairs*) So it does.

Paillardin He's coming up the ladder. Why aren't you at school, young man?

Maxime (*off*) I can explain everything, uncle.

Paillardin I hope you can.

Maxime, wearing a hat, appears at the window with a cigarette in his mouth. He climbs in and moves downstage

Paillardin moves downstage to his R

Maxime Good morning, M'sieur Pinglet. Morning, uncle. (*He takes his hat off, then notices Paillardin's eye. He looks again, then puts his hat on the desk*) I say, uncle, wherever did you get that shiner?

Paillardin That's not the point. The point is, why aren't you at school?

Maxime Ah. That. I was just going to tell you. Last night. I must have forgotten to wind up ...

Pinglet Wind what up?

Maxime My watch, m'sieur. So I got the time wrong last night and when I got to the Lycée yesterday evening, I was too late. The gates were locked!

Paillardin What on earth are you talking about? Is this some sort of joke?

Maxime I promise you. I've never been more serious in my life.

Pinglet (*aside*) Not a bad little actor. He was tucked up with Victoire in the Free Trade Hotel.

Maxime blows smoke in his uncle's face

Paillardin (*coughing*) So why didn't you come straight back home?

Maxime Oh, uncle. It was much too late, and you were out, weren't you? And I didn't want to upset auntie.

Paillardin Don't beat about the bush, boy! Where did you spend the night?

Maxime They gave me a room, at the *Continental*.

Paillardin Are you sure?

Maxime Do you doubt my word?

Pinglet (*aside*) Nothing like a little philosophy to teach you contempt for the truth.

Maxime And when I got to the Lycée Stanislas this morning the head-master wouldn't let me in without a letter from you, uncle.

Paillardin We'll see about that.

Marcelle (*off*) Henri! Henri!

Pinglet and Paillardin turn to the door

Maxime (*aside*) Thank God he never recognized me at the hotel!

Paillardin That sounds very much like my wife. (*He moves downstairs*)

Maxime sits on the stool

(*To Marcelle*) Here I am my dear.

Paillardin deafens Pinglet as he shouts to Marcelle. He then passes in front of Pinglet and moves to the c of the UR door. Pinglet moves L a little on the platform

Marcelle (*off*) All right. Open up.

Paillardin Can't be done. Madame Pinglet's got the key. I had to come up through the window. I'm here with good old Pinglet.

Marcelle (*off*) Oh, are you . . .?

Pinglet Good morning to you, Madame Paillardin.

Marcelle (*off*) Oh. Good morning to you, M'sieur Pinglet.

Pinglet (*greeting Marcelle as though he could see her*) And how are we feeling this morning? I do hope you slept well.

Marcelle (*off*) Only so-so, I'm afraid. I had rather a restless night.

Pinglet Oh, poor old you. I'm so sorry.

Paillardin Talk about restless nights! What about me? You know what happened to me?

Marcelle (*off*) Not really. What?

Paillardin You won't believe this. You know the Free Trade Hotel?

Marcelle (*off, positively*) Of course I don't! Never heard of it!

Pinglet No! Never heard of it! Never in our lives. What on earth's the Free Trade Hotel? I've no idea where it is even.

Marcelle (*off*) Neither have I. No idea at all!

Paillardin Of course you don't know it. It's an extremely dubious hotel. Why on earth *should* you know it?

Pinglet Exactly. Dubious place! (*He laughs*) How on earth would we know it?

Marcelle (*off, almost at the same time*) How on earth would we know it?

Maxime How on earth would we know it?

Paillardin and Pinglet turn to look at Maxime who looks out front

Paillardin Well. Let me tell you about this nightmarish hotel. Half a minute. It's not very convenient talking to you through a door. I'll just hop out of the window and come round by the garden. With you in a jiffy.

Marcelle (*off*) Oh, all right.

Paillardin (*to Pinglet*) Do you mind? We had a few cross words yesterday. East wind blowing, you know. I'd like to make peace with my wife. (*He moves to the window as he talks*)

Pinglet (*ushering Paillardin out*) Well, of course. Make it up at once.

Paillardin (*to Maxime*) Out you go, my boy. I'll follow you down.

Maxime disappears out of the window

(*To Pinglet*) Want to join me?

Paillardin exits out of the window

Pinglet What? Me? Oh no. I'll stay here. I'll stay. (*Aside*) Thanks very much. You want to ruin my alibi? (*He moves to open the door but then goes back to the window*) Put the ladder away. Don't forget! (*He closes the window and moves downstairs*)

Paillardin (*off*) Oh, very well.

Marcelle (*off*) Has my husband gone down?

Pinglet The coast's clear. Pull the bolt. (*He unlocks the door*)

Marcells unbolts the door. Pinglet opens it

Marcelle (*in the doorway*) What did he say?

Pinglet He doesn't know a thing! He's not at all suspicious.

Marcelle Oh, thank God!

Pinglet (*in agitation*) He didn't see anything. Except your dress. Your puce dress. That's all he saw of you last night. Burn it! Bury it! But, by all that's holy, don't ever let him get a glimpse of it.

Marcelle I'm glad you told me. I'll see to it at once.

Pinglet He's on his way round. Get back home and change. (*He shuts the door in her face*)

Marcelle (*off*) Aagh!

Pinglet The bolt! Shoot the bolt!

Sound of the bolt closing

(*Moving to the chaise*) Safe at last! (*He sits*) But I'm beginning to get bored in here. (*He gets up*) I hope to God my wife comes back soon and sets me free. I know her sister's ill, but I can't stay in here for ever!

Victoire (*off*) M'sieur! Are you there, m'sieur?

Pinglet Yes, Victoire! What is it?

Victoire (*off*) Telegram for you, m'sieur.

Pinglet Push it under the door. (*He rises and moves to the door*)
Victoire (*off*) Here it comes!

The telegram slides under the door. Pinglet picks it up

Pinglet Probably from the hornet! (*He opens it*) From the hornet's sister!
(*He reads it*) "We're extremely worried. Angelique didn't arrive for
dinner. We waited for her in vain." She waited in vain for Madame
Pinglet! Lucky old her! "Is she ill? Telegraph at once!" What's it all mean?
(*He moves* C) My wife isn't with her sister? Let me see, let me see. Last
night she set out for . . . (*his face lights up*) could she have been kidnapped?
(*Disappointed*) Afraid not. These days acts of heroism are far too rare.
Could it be . . . could it possibly be . . . (*he starts to laugh*) that Madame
Pinglet . . . her too! She set out on a little adventure? (*He stops laughing*)
It's not possible. Unless she had a blind date! Literally!
Mme Pinglet (*off, in a tremulous voice*) Pinglet . . . Are you there, Pinglet?
Pinglet (*depressed*) I knew it was too good to last. (*He quickly moves* UL)
She sounds a bit shaky. Now's the time to get out of bed!

He goes into his bedroom, leaving the door open

Mme Pinglet (*off, unbolting the door*) Oh, Pinglet. My dear, dear Pinglet!
My little Benoit!

*Mme Pinglet enters wearing a torn dress, a hat with no goggle and carrying
her coat and umbrella. She has a huge black eye*

What a night! My God, what a night I've had! (*She leans on the door,
slamming it shut, then staggers behind the armchair and drops her coat on it.
She then staggers back to the door*) Benoit. My dearest husband. (*She puts
her umbrella in the stand*) Where are you? (*She staggers* L)
Pinglet (*off*) What? Who's there? Who's waking me up?
Mme Pinglet It's me. And I'm still alive. (*She moves* UC *to the balustrade and
stands on the platform*) Thanks be to God!
Pinglet (*off*) For small mercies!
Mme Pinglet When you know what I've suffered. . . . Oh, Benoit! When you
hear of the terrible dangers I've been through. . . . While you were safely
tucked up in bed. Where are you?
Pinglet Here!

*He appears at the door of his bedroom, leaving the door open. He yawns
heavily*

Mme Pinglet (*moving* L *to* UR *of his door*) I'm so happy to see you again, my
darling! (*She attempts to smother him with kisses*)
Pinglet (*fending her off*) Any particular reason?
Mme Pinglet What a night! What a night I've had. . . . What troubles and
tribulations!
Pinglet (*aside*) That same old song! (*He takes his wife's head in his hands*)
Good grief. What a shiner!
Mme Pinglet Oh, Pinglet! Pinglet! You nearly lost me!
Pinglet (*calmly, to the audience*) *Nearly*?

Mme Pinglet I swear it. Doesn't that distress you?

Pinglet Of course. (*Aside*) So near and yet so far.

Mme Pinglet Oh, my dear. A terrible accident . . . (*she puts her* L *arm round his neck*) *nearly* snatched me from you!

Pinglet Don't tell me that again. It's breaking my heart . . .

Mme Pinglet You're such a good, kind man.

Pinglet takes her to the chaise and pushes her so that she falls in the C *of it. He then sits on the extreme* L *end*

I took a cab, as you know to Ville d'Avray. Everything was going so well. We were quite contented, all three of us.

Pinglet All three?

Mme Pinglet The cabbie, the horse and your dear, devoted wife. And then a train whistled . . . and the horse bolted, terrified, and . . .

Pinglet I nearly lost you!

Mme Pinglet The cabbie dragged on the reins. He tried to stop the horse. Impossible? Picture me, Pinglet! Flying across the countryside, galloping at breakneck speed. Not a soul about. No one to help us. It's in such moments of terror, Benoit, that one thinks of one's husband.

Pinglet I think of you in moments of terror, too.

Mme Pinglet I said to myself. . . . (*With emotion*) If only he were with me now!

Pinglet You're too kind!

Mme Pinglet Anyway. You weren't there. So I lost my head. I opened the cab door . . . and leapt! (*She rises, staggers* DR, *then drops to her knees and up again in one, inelegant movement*)

Pinglet Leapt?

Mme Pinglet Leapt into the void! Nearly to my destruction! (*She sinks into the armchair*)

Pinglet *Nearly?*

Mme Pinglet After that . . . I remember nothing! All I know is that I awoke about dawn, in a rude peasant hut. Among rude peasants who seemed pleased to see me alive.

Pinglet (*aside*) Not rude. Just dense!

Mme Pinglet But they were good, kind people. I'm sorry I only had a hundred francs in my purse. I wanted to give them all that we possess.

Pinglet That might have been over generous.

Mme Pinglet But they saved my life!

Pinglet (*between clenched teeth*) Exactly!

Mme Pinglet And so this morning when I was feeling well enough to travel, they took me in a rustic cart . . . as far as the Arc de Triomphe! I got a cab and here I am!

Pinglet (*calmly*) How terrible.

Mme Pinglet (*crying*) Oh, Pinglet! When I think of it. When I remember that ghastly moment. Your poor little wife. (*She sobs, returns to the chaise and leans against Pinglet, trying to embrace him*)

Pinglet (*shrinking away*) Brace up! There's nothing for you to cry about.

Mme Pinglet Poor Pinglet! What would you have done if you'd lost me?

Pinglet (*taking her in his arms*) I tell you one thing. I'd never have married again!

Victoire enters UR *with a salver and begins to move* DR *to the desk*

Victoire The post, madame.
Mme Pinglet (*pointing to the sofa*) Just put it down here, Victoire.

Victoire moves R *of the chaise, putting the letters on the* R *end. She holds the salver*

Pinglet I'll get dressed.

He rises, exits UL *and changes into his smoking jacket*

Mme Pinglet Oh yes. Off you go! I feel quite dizzy. It must be the reaction. What I need is a nice hot bath! (*To Victoire*) Go and run it! (*She takes her hat off*)
Victoire Madame, I don't know whether you have noticed. But you have an absolutely terrific black eye!
Mme Pinglet It's none of your business. It's my eye. And put a good dollop of lime flower oil in it.
Victoire In madame's eye?
Mme Pinglet No. In madame's bath. (*She throws her hat at Victoire, who catches it on the salver*)
Victoire Yes, Madame.

Victoire exits, also taking Mme Pinglet's coat from the armchair

Mme Pinglet Servants nowadays. (*She opens a letter*)
Pinglet (*off, singing*) Comes my love, with little fairy footsteps!
　　　　　　　　Comes my love, tip-toeing o'er the grass!
Mme Pinglet (*reading the letter*) What's all this? *The Department of Public Morality*. What on earth can the Department of Public Morality want with me? (*She reads aloud*) You are hereby summoned to present yourself at this office in connection with the case you are concerned in and to bring proof of your identity! What can it mean? (*She reads more*) To Madame Pinglet who was discovered in a compromising position with a certain Monsieur Paillardin during police investigations last night at the Free Trade Hotel. (*In astonishment*) Me! Police investigations! With Paillar ... in the Free ... Trade ... Hotel ... It's a madman! A maniac! I've had a letter from a maniac! (*In agitation*) What's it say again? (*She tries to read it*) The letter's an hallucination! Am I going mad?

Pinglet enters in his smoking jacket. He carries a boot in his L *hand*

Pinglet Disaster!
Mme Pinglet Yes!
Pinglet A button's come off my boot! (*He pulls the bell-pull*)
Mme Pinglet Thank God you're here!
Pinglet What's the matter?
Mme Pinglet (*deeply disturbed*) This letter! Am I going mad? It says ... It

makes ... The most appalling suggestions. Take it, Pinglet. Read it! (*She gives him the letter*)

Pinglet (*glancing at it*) Oh, my God! From the police ... So soon?

Pinglet Go on! Read the dreadful thing!

Pinglet (*aside*) Now we're in the soup! (*He moves* DL *as he reads*) You are hereby summoned ... proof of identity ... to Madame Pinglet who was discovered in a compromising position with a certain Monsieur Paillardin last night at the Free Trade Hotel.

Mme Pinglet That's me! Me! *I* was discovered in a compromising position with Monsieur Paillardin!

Pinglet (*slamming the summons on the* DL *desk*) So! You admit it!

Mme Pinglet (*flabbergasted*) What?

Pinglet Miserable woman! Your sins have found you out. Caught in a compromising position with my best friend. (*He hits the table with his boot*) Messalina!

Mme Pinglet No. No. I'm your little Angelique! You don't believe ...

Pinglet Get thee behind me. (*He moves to the chaise, grabs her by her* R *hand and swings her around to his* L, *forcing her onto her knees*)

Mme Pinglet But Pinglet!

Pinglet (*furiously*) So, Cleopatra of Old Nile! What did you get up to with Paillardin, eh? What tricks?

Mme Pinglet (*rising*) Nothing! Absolutely nothing. It's all a bad dream!

Pinglet (*picking up the summons and putting it in his pocket, then talking threateningly into her* L, *then her* R *ear*) So that summons is a dream, is it? I didn't know the police were given to day dreaming. (*Dramatically*) The game's up, madame! You'd better make a clean breast of it. Admit it!

Mme Pinglet Pinglet! You misjudge me terribly!

Pinglet (*in a terrible voice*) *Admit it!* (*He takes her by the wrist*)

Mme Pinglet You don't want me to admit something that's not true?

Pinglet (*brandishing his boot*) I don't care about that. *Admit it!* (*He forces her on the ground*)

Mme Pinglet (*on her knees*) Spare me, Pinglet!

Pinglet raises his boot as if to strike her

Aaaaah!

Victoire enters UR, *leaving the door open. She stays in the doorway*

Victoire Did someone call?

Pinglet (*calmly*) Oh, Victoire. Could you sew a button on my boot? (*He throws the boot to her*) And make sure it stays on this time! The last one popped off.

Victoire (*backing towards the door*) Certainly, m'sieur.

Victoire exits

Pinglet (*furiously*) And you were the woman I trusted.

He threatens Mme Pinglet and she leans backwards. But then she rebounds and grabs him by the jacket as he moves R. *She is dragged along the floor*

I had faith in you. I used to boast to my friends.

He slaps her hands and she lets go. Then he picks her up by her collar, to a kneeling position

"All right," I'd say, "My wife is a sour-faced, stunningly boring old battle axe, but at least she's faithful!"

He pushes her and she falls back on the floor

I can't even pay you that compliment any more. At your age! (*He moves up the stairs*)

Mme Pinglet picks herself up with the aid of a tassel on the chaise and follows him, catching Pinglet up on the stairs. She falls on her knees again

Mme Pinglet I tell you. It's lies. All lies!

Pinglet I see it all now! I see why you locked me in here. So you could satisfy your filthy lust with the architect next door.

Mme Pinglet I never dreamed . . .

Pinglet I suppose your poor ill sister lives at the Free Trade Hotel. A place of ill repute in the rue de Provence!

Mme Pinglet I've never been there in my life. Why do you say it's in the rue de Provence?

Pinglet (*taking the summons from his pocket*) It says so in the summons. (*He looks*) Oh no! It doesn't!

Mme Pinglet I've told you the truth! The whole truth! Nothing but the truth! The horse bolted. Those poor peasants cared for me!

Pinglet And where are these poor peasants, eh? Tell me that.

Mme Pinglet (*rising*) In their village. I suppose.

Pinglet (*putting the summons away*) And where is their village?

Mme Pinglet Oh, God. I should've asked them. But we'd travelled so far and I never dreamt.

Pinglet (*turning to the window, in disbelief*) Huh!

Mme Pinglet Listen! I've just thought. Paillardin! Paillardin will tell you the truth. He's accused with me. Paillardin can explain everything! (*She becomes entangled in the palm at the bottom of the stairs*)

Pinglet We shall see. (*He looks out of the window*) Speak of the devil! Here comes your precious paramour. Walking across the garden in a particularly brazen manner. (*He opens the window and calls*) Paillardin! Paillardin!

Paillardin (*off*) What's the matter?

Pinglet (*severely*) Come up here a moment! I want to talk to you!

Paillardin (*off*) What do you want to say?

Pinglet Come up and you'll find out! (*He closes the window and moves downstage*) And as for you, madame. When your accomplice is here I don't want you to breathe a word. Not a gesture. No signals. You understand? Complete silence in the face of the Court!

Mme Pinglet (*praying dramatically, her hands raised to heaven*) How long? How long, oh Lord . . . Shall thy innocent ones suffer? (*She staggers to the L end of the chaise*)

As Paillardin enters and stands below the stairs

(*Falling to her knees, head on the chaise*) Lighten our darkness, I pray you. And bring forth the truth!

Pinglet sits on his stool on the rostrum

Paillardin (*puzzled*) What do you want?

Pinglet (*seriously*) You may approach the Seat of Judgement.

Paillardin (*laughing*) The Seat of Judgement? What're you playing at?

Mme Pinglet Oh, Paillardin. Tell him ...

Pinglet (*making a warning gesture*) Be careful, madame! No hints! Let justice take its course. (*To Paillardin*) Now then, Paillardin. Perhaps you'll tell us where you spent last night.

Paillardin (*moving downstage to* L *of the armchair*) Last night? I was at the Free Trade Hotel. Of course.

Mme Pinglet (*astonished*) Where? (*She rises and moves towrds the* C)

Paillardin Two-two-oh, rue de Provence.

Pinglet (*triumphantly*) You have heard the evidence, madame.

Mme Pinglet (*astonished*) Am I going mad? Is it possible that I ...? With ...? Did ...? Oh no! Not that! Never that! (*She collapses on the chaise*)

Paillardin (*aside*) What's eating them?

Pinglet (*to Paillardin*) And who were you with at the Free Trade Hotel? Come along, m'sieur! Don't fence with me! Just answer the question.

Paillardin I was alone.

Pinglet (*in a terrible voice*) Don't lie to me, m'sieur. You were with my wife!

Paillardin What?

Pinglet The game's up, Paillardin! You are my wife's lover!

Paillardin (*in astonishment*) Me?

Mme Pinglet (*to her husband*) You see!

Pinglet Silence, madame! (*He moves downstairs to Paillardin, the summons in his hand*)

Paillardin Very funny, Pinglet. Extremely humorous! Of course you're joking.

Pinglet Am I? Am I joking? Read that! (*He gives him the summons*) Is that a joke?

Paillardin What've you got there? (*He reads it*) To Madame Pinglet who was found in a compromising position with Monsieur Paillardin during police investigations last night at the Free Trade Hotel. (*He starts to laugh and slaps Pinglet on the back*) Oh, delicious! Very comic. Highly comical. You are a terrible old practical joker.

Pinglet A joker? Do I look like a joker? (*He leans on the end of the chaise in a dramatic pose*)

Mme Pinglet My husband has got the idea that I could. ... That I did. ... With *you*! Yes. I promise you!

Paillardin Me? Your lover! (*In fits of laughter*) What a joke. What a wonderful joke!

Pinglet Don't try and laugh it off, m'sieur.

Paillardin But you can't be serious. You honestly think that *I* ...? You need your head examined! (*Amongst fits of laughter, he sits on the armchair*)

Pinglet Let me remind you. The summons proves it. (*He waves the summons at Paillardin*)

Paillardin Paillardin Me. ... The lover of. ... Now listen to me, my dear fellow. Be reasonable. I mean, I've got absolutely nothing against your wife. For all I know she may cook a very tolerable blanquette de veau. She may do reasonable plain sewing. I'm sure she's a dab hand at potting meat. But me ... hanky-panky with Madame Pinglet! I mean, look at her! I mean look at her!

Pinglet I think you'd better not insult my wife, just at the moment.

Mme Pinglet Is he insulting me? (*She rises, moves* DL *and sits in despair. She bangs her head on the desk and moans*)

Pinglet Oh yes, madame! That's the sort of man he is. He put you on a pedestal and now he's knocking you off. He squeezed the juice out of you and now he casts you aside like an old bit of dried up lemon.

Paillardin The whole thing's ridiculous!

Pinglet Oh yes. (*He indicates the summons*) Then how do you explain that?

Paillardin (*rising and putting the summons on the table*) I don't know. Someone's got a weird sense of humour. And the proof of that is—why haven't I got a summons too? If I was involved in your wife's so-called love affairs, wouldn't they have summoned me as well? And I've had nothing! Nothing, you hear? All right. Until I get a summons like that I shall deny all the charges. And I'll go on denying them while there's breath left in my body! (*He runs out of breath*)

Victoire enters UR *with a letter and Pinglet's boot. She leaves the door open and addresses Pinglet*

Victoire Excuse me, m'sieur. A policeman just arrived with this for Monsieur Paillardin.

Paillardin (*opening the letter*) What on earth is it?

Pinglet (*triumphantly*) You know perfectly well!

Paillardin (*reading, very quietly*) To Monsieur Paillardin who was discovered in a compromising position with Madame Pinglet during the police investigations last night at the Free Trade Hotel.

Pinglet Hasn't that rather taken the wind out of your sails?

Paillardin (*in astonishment*) This is ridiculous!

Mme Pinglet (*despairingly*) Destiny's got it in for us! What can we do about it?

Pinglet Do you still deny it?

Paillardin (*in astonishment*) I simply can't understand it!

Victoire Your boot, m'sieur. (*She gives it to Pinglet*)

Pinglet Oh, thanks. (*To Paillardin*) Miserable! Miserable sinner!

Victoire What've *I* done, m'sieur?

Pinglet Not you. Clear off. (*He puts the boot back on her salver*)

Victoire Very well, m'sieur.

As Victoire exits Marcelle enters in a blue dress and moves between Paillardin and Pinglet. Victoire closes the door

Pinglet Madame.

Paillardin Marcelle!

Pinglet You came at a most convenient moment. You see that wretched man?

Marcelle (*in astonishment*) I see my husband.

Pinglet That's him. He's my wife's lover!

Marcelle Him!

Paillardin ⎱ (*together*)⎰ Oh, my God! (*Paillardin turns away* R *and puts the*
Mme Pinglet ⎰   ⎱ *summons on the armchair*)

Pinglet (*aside, to Marcelle*) There's not a word of truth in it. Just pass out in my arms. (*He puts his arms out behind her*)

Marcelle Right. Oh! (*She falls straight through his arms to the floor*)

Paillardin But it's a lie. All lies. Oh, my God!

Pinglet kneels and lifts Marcelle's head up

(*Noticing Marcelle now and kneeling to her* R) You must be mad to tell her that! Marcelle! Marcelle, my dear little wife! (*He slaps her hands*) Quick. Smelling salts immediately!

Mme Pinglet I've got some. (*She quickly moves* DR *and hurdles over Marcelle*)

Mme Pinglet exits DR. *Paillardin, rocked by the wind she makes, rises and follows her into the bedroom*

Marcelle (*opening her eyes, and in a very faint voice*) Where am I?

Pinglet (*very quickly and quietly*) They both got summonses. From the police. So to get us out of a hole, I accused *them*! You twig?

Marcelle I twig!

Paillardin rushes in with the smelling salts and moves R *of Pinglet*

Pinglet Faint again. Go on, faint!

Marcells lets her head fall back on Pinglet's shoulder

Mme Pinglet returns

Paillardin (*threatening Pinglet with the bottle as though it were a revolver*) M'sieur, your conduct is unworthy of a gentleman! (*He holds the bottle under Pinglet's nose, then Marcelle's*)

Pinglet You're a fine one to talk! (*In a business like tone*) Don't hold it up there. You'll corrode her poor little neglected nostrils. Give it to me. (*He snatches the bottle and hands it to his wife, who takes a sniff and lurches back. She then takes the bottle and gets up*)

Paillardin She looks terrible! My God. What a tragedy! Water! We need water! (*He breaks* R *in a flap*)

Mme Pinglet looks for water DL

Pinglet (*under his breath*) That's quite enough, Marcelle. Don't overdo it!

Marcelle All right. (*She pretends to revive*) Aaah!

Pinglet helps Marcelle to the chaise and she lies down

Mme Pinglet She's coming back to life!

Paillardin (*to Marcelle*) Marcelle. (*He moves* L *and kneels on the chaise*) I beg you. Don't believe a word he says.

Mme Pinglet (*moving above the chaise and sitting upstage*) It's lies! All lies ...

Pinglet (*leaning towards Marcelle*) They were only caught together. In a compromising position. In a police raid—in a hotel of ill repute!

Marcelle (*sitting up without conviction*) How horrible.

Paillardin and Mme Pinglet rise and face front, Paillardin on the L

(*Turning to Pinglet*) Shall I faint again?

Pinglet (*under his breath*) No. Get very angry.

Marcelle (*under her breath*) Oh, very well. (*She shouts at Paillardin*) Aaah!

Paillardin moves L *a pace*

Mme Pinglet (*in fright*) She's absolutely livid! (*She gradually moves* L)

Paillardin (*moving to Marcelle*) Marcelle. Please. You can't believe everything you read in summonses. (*He tries to take her arm*)

Marcelle Take your hands off me, Paillardin. I suppose she (*she points at Mme Pinglet*) was one of your so-called spooks!

Pinglet Oh yes. For your husband it was knocking ghosts. For my wife it was a run-away cab horse. (*He moves* DR, *below the armchair*) And by a strange coincidence they both came home with black eyes! And they expect us to believe that they got their two shiners on separate occasions!

Marcelle (*rising*) *Two* shiners!

Paillardin All right. We've had quite enough of this! You're both sure that we were caught having hanky-panky in a dubious hotel ...

Pinglet Quite, quite sure!

Paillardin All right. We'll all four of us go off to the Police Station and see if the Inspector identifies us.

Pinglet and Marcelle look at each other

Pinglet | (*together*) | No! Oh no!
Marcelle | | We couldn't possibly do that.

Mme Pinglet That's it! What a wonderful idea! (*She moves behind the chaise, takes Pinglet by the* L *arm and swings him over the chaise to* UC) We'll all go to the police station!

Paillardin takes Marcelle's R *arm and brings her* UCR. *Marcelle hangs onto the banister with her* L *arm. Mme Pinglet takes her husband by the* L *arm. He too clings onto the banister*

Pinglet | (*together*) | No! It's a terrible idea! Really quite stupid!
Marcelle | | Oh no!

Paillardin Oh yes! You brought the accusation! You'll go through with it! Only the Inspector can settle this once and for all. Down to the police station ...

Victoire enters and announces—

Victoire Monsieur Mathieu! (*She moves* R *of the door*)

Pinglet ⎫ (*together*) Him!
Marcelle ⎭

Mathieu enters

Mathieu What a night, my friends! What a terrible night!

Pinglet ⎫ (*together, to the audience*) Oh, my God! (*Pinglet moves a pace*
Marcelle ⎭   *downstage*)

Mathieu (*giving his hat and coat to Victoire*) Good morning to you, Pinglet.

Pinglet Is it good? Is it a good morning for you? (*He moves to Mathieu*) Go
and wait for me in my room on this good morning. (*He pushes Mathieu
upstage of the chaise towards the door* UL) We're rather busy!

Mathieu Yes, of course. Good morning Madame Paillardin. Good morning, Madame Pinglet. (*He stops dead as he notices her eye*)

Pinglet exits to the bedroom

I say, has something happened to your eye? (*He steps up to Mme Pinglet*)

Mme Pinglet Oh no! Nothing at all.

Mathieu If only you knew what happened to me since I left here yesterday
evening!

Pinglet emerges from the bedroom

Pinglet (*pushing Mathieu to the door*) You can tell us all about that later.

Mathieu (*turning back*) My daughters and I spent the night in the cell ...

Pinglet (*quickly*) Sel ... ect Hotel. (*He turns him round*) Take no notice of
this fellow. He stutters. ... Can't make head or tail of a word he says.

Mathieu What do you mean ... stutter? I'm not stuttering.

*Pinglet moves downstage behind the chaise for his next line, then turns back to
Mathieu to pull him in the bedroom*

Pinglet (*despairingly, aside*) Please God! Let it rain!

Mathieu moves R *at exactly the same time so that they cross, Pinglet ending
up in the bedroom once more*

Mathieu (*moving downstage*) Happily they realized who we were this
morning and we were given our freedom!

Pinglet re-emerges

Pinglet (*rushing to Mathieu*) That's all right then. Come on. For God's
sake. Get into my room. In there! In there! (*He takes him by the shoulders*)

Mathieu I've had quite enough of Paris. We're taking the first train back to
Dieppe.

Pinglet (*pushing him towards the* UR *door*) Dieppe! Then it's that way. Over
there! Over there! Out there! Out there!

Mathieu Not yet.

Pinglet (*pushing him* UL) Oh! All right. Then it's that way. In there!

*Pinglet pushes Mathieu into his bedroom and closes the door. He turns in
relief to the others*

Mathieu opens the door and comes out

Mathieu What about the rest of you? How did you get on there last night?

Victoire reacts, then exits quickly with Mathieu's hat and coat

Pinglet I slept like a log. Thank you very much! (*He seizes Mathieu by the throat*)

Mathieu I say. Careful!

Mathieu turns and makes a dignified exit into the bedroom. Pinglet closes the door

Mme Pinglet (*to Paillardin*) What do you suppose he meant by, "How did you get on there last night?"

Pinglet (*moving* UCL) Oh, didn't you know? It's typical! Dieppe dialect. When you want to ask someone how they slept ... in Dieppe you always say, "How did you get on there last night?"

Mme Pinglet How very interesting. I never knew that!

Paillardin Right! We're off to see the Inspector.

He and Madame Pinglet take the others by the hands. Pinglet and Marcelle hold on to the balcony

Pinglet }
Marcelle } (*together*) No! No! (*They resist*)

Paillardin gets his hand on the UR *door handle and opens it*

Victoire staggers in

Paillardin, the Pinglets and Marcelle fall over as Paillardin pulls the door back

Victoire stands to the R *of the door and announces*

Victoire Inspector Boucard of The Department of Public Morality.

All The Inspector!

Paillardin Excellent. Just in time!

Pinglet and Marcelle quickly move DL *to the desk*

Boucard enters and gives his umbrella to Victoire, then puts his gloves inside his hat and gives them to her too

Pinglet (*aside*) Our goose is cooked! (*He turns his back on Boucard*)

Paillardin   }   {Come along in, Inspector.
Mme Pinglet } (*together, to Boucard*) {This way, Inspector.

Paillardin moves downstage beckoning to Boucard

Mme Pinglet quickly moves DR *to Boucard, then moves to the* C, *knocking into the armchair*

Boucard Monsieur Paillardin!

Paillardin I'm Paillardin.

Victoire exits UR *with the hat and umbrella*

Boucard Forgive me, m'sieur. I didn't recognize you at first. After all, you were all covered with soot!

Paillardin *I* was?

Boucard But I remember you perfectly now.

Paillardin \
Mme Pinglet ⌋ (*together*) What's that?

Pinglet (*under his breath to Marcelle*) He remembers him! That's not bad.

Paillardin You remember me, m'sieur?

Boucard Of course. You're the fellow I caught with Madame Pinglet at the Free Trade Hotel.

Mme Pinglet (*moving in a pace*) Me? You caught me?

Paillardin Me? With her?

Boucard (*turning to Madame Pinglet*) Madame Pinglet. Of course!

Mme Pinglet Of course I'm Madame Pinglet!

Boucard (*moving to her* R) You must forgive me. Last night I could hardly see you for lace.

Mme Pinglet Me?

Boucard But now I can identify you perfectly. We get pretty skilled at identification you know, in the Department of Public Morality.

All What?

Mme Pinglet You can identify me?

Boucard (*facing downstage*) She's a bit of an eyesore!

Pinglet (*delighted, to Marcelle*) He can identify her. He's a sleuth in a million!

Paillardin (*moving downstage a pace*) M'sieur. You can't possibly identify us. For the plain and simple reason that you never saw us in the Free Trade Hotel.

Boucard (*turning to Paillardin*) And I suppose I never arrested you! Never questioned you! Never let you out on bail!

Paillardin It wasn't us. It was a couple of jokers impersonating us.

Boucard Anyway. It's of absolutely no importance.

Paillardin \
Mme Pinglet ⌋ (*together*) Of no importance!

Boucard I'm only sorry that my fool of a secretary sent out those summonses. Now I know who you are, m'sieur, we can consider, the matter closed. M'sieur, are you not M'sieur Paillardin, Architect and Learned Expert appointed by the Court in Building and Allied Matters?

Paillardin I don't see what that's got to do with it. It's immaterial!

Boucard For you, perhaps. But not for me! It's a bit of luck, running into you. Here's the problem. I've bought this little property in the country, and the beams! Riddled with woodworm!

Mme Pinglet sits DR

And the dry rot . . .!

Paillardin (*impatiently*) M'sieur. It doesn't matter about your dry rot! What matters is last night!

Boucard I told you. Don't worry about it. You've got a permanent address?

Means of support? A bulging bank account? Then you're of no concern whatever to the Department of Public Morality.

Paillardin But we're of concern to that lady and gentleman! (*He points to Pinglet and Marcelle*)

Boucard (*bowing to them*) M'sieur! Madame!

They return his bows with their backs still to him

Paillardin (*moving upstage*) Our respective spouses took your summonses to mean that last night we actually. . . . Well! I demand my rights. You must make it clear that you can't possibly identify us!

Boucard I keep on telling you that!

Paillardin No you don't. You say you can't remember our faces. At least tell them that you didn't arrest *us*!

Boucard You're making things very difficult for me.

Paillardin Try and remember! Take a good look at us.

Mme Pinglet If you can't remember the woman's face, think of her size, her figure perhaps.

Pinglet masks Marcelle from Boucard as he turns to look L

Boucard Well, there is one thing I do remember!

Everyone listens

The female person in question was sporting a somewhat vulgar and ostentatious dress, puce in colour.

Mme Pinglet And I haven't got such a thing!

Marcelle (*positively*) Nor have I! (*She takes a step forward, then quickly turns back*)

Pinglet (*under his breath*) Shut up!

Paillardin (*to Marcelle*) No one's talking about you!

Boucard (*moving to Madame Pinglet*) I'm sorry, madame. That's the best I can do. My recollection's extremely vague . . .

Paillardin Then set up an inquiry.

Boucard An inquiry?

Paillardin You arrested a lot of people last night. Let's see if any of them can identify us.

Boucard Brilliant! I've got a list. (*He takes out his notebook and tries to read it, first holding it far away and then holding it near, with his glasses raised*)

Paillardin (*impatiently taking the book and reading aloud from it*) Let me have a look.

Boucard looks over his shoulder

Gaston, the Bull of Boulogne. Never met him. Adele Dubois, known as the "Flea". Bastien Morillian, hairdresser. M'sieur le Juge de . . .

Boucard Better not read that out!

Paillardin Oh, very well. Monsieur Mathieu and his alleged daughters.

Mme Pinglet (*rising*) Mathieu! Which Mathieu? We've got a Mathieu here this morning.

Pinglet (*aside*) Damn!
Boucard Here?

Paillardin gives the book back to Boucard, who again attempts to read it himself

Mme Pinglet In this very apartment! And he has no less than four daughters!
Paillardin And he spent the night in the cell . . .
Pinglet (*moving below the chaise*) Select Hotel.
Paillardin No. No. You said that. He meant in chokey.

As Boucard turns L, *Pinglet turns away*

Boucard Must be one and the same individual.
Mme Pinglet Well, for goodness sake. Let's ask him. (*She moves above the chaise to call Mathieu*) Mathieu!

Paillardin follows her. At the same time, Boucard moves R *of the armchair to the platform too*

Mathieu!
Marcelle (*moving* R *of Pinglet, under her breath*) The ground's opening beneath our feet! (*She moves to the armchair and sits*)
Pinglet I wish it would!
Mme Pinglet (*opening Pinglet's door*) Come out, M'sieur Mathieu. (*She knocks on the door, then moves* DL)
Paillardin (*calling*) Come out! Come out!

Mathieu enters and stands in the doorway

Mathieu What is it now?
Paillardin (*moving to Mathieu and pulling him*) Come along. Don't be nervous.
Mathieu My God, the police again! What've I done now? (*He tries to escape*)

Paillardin holds him

Paillardin ⎫   ⎧M'sieur Mathieu! You can solve the mystery!
Mme Pinglet ⎬ (*together*) ⎨M'sieur Mathieu! Only you can save us!
Boucard ⎭   ⎩Yes, M'sieur Mathieu! You can jog my memory.
                                        (*He moves nearer Mathieu*)
Mathieu Don't all speak at once!
Pinglet (*aside*) And the awful thing is . . . he's not stuttering.
Paillardin Last night you were in the Free Trade Hotel.

Mathieu moves L *of Boucard as he steps off the platform to the* UL *corner of the chaise*

Mathieu Where I was arrested for no apparent reason. With my daughters. Thrown into the cells! Me, a barrister-at-law!
Paillardin (*moving* L *of Mathieu*) No one cares about all that. The point is, did you see Madame Pinglet and me there at all?

Mathieu You and Madame Pinglet? Certainly not.
Mme Pinglet (*to Boucard*) There! You see?
Mathieu When I think of my poor children. Up till now they've had no sort of criminal record ...
Paillardin I told you. No one's interested in you. The point is, did you see somebody else?
Mathieu Of course I saw somebody else! (*He sits*)
Boucard ⎫
Mme Pinglet ⎬ (*together*) Who? Tell us who?
Paillardin ⎭
Marcelle (*to the audience*) Here it comes!
Pinglet The game's up!
Mathieu (*to Pinglet, laughing*) Listen to this, Pinglet. They're asking me who I saw at the hotel last night!
Pinglet (*with a forced smile*) Oh, really?
Mathieu And shall I tell them who I saw? Shall I?

Pinglet tugs at the tail of his coat

Leave my coat tails alone, why don't you? (*He rises and moves* L, *dragging Pinglet along the chaise*)

Pinglet lets go of his tails

Boucard moves around the R *end of the chaise to the* DR *corner of it*

Mathieu (*to Madame Pinglet*) Well I'll tell you. I saw ... I saw quite clearly ...

Sound of a thunder clap, then pouring rain

I s ... s ... s ... s ...

Mme Pinglet What's the matter with the man?
Marcelle (*aside*) He's stuttering!

Pinglet leaps onto the chaise and holds his arms to heaven

Pinglet Rain! Blessed rain! Thanks be to God! My prayers are answered!
Boucard (*moving a pace downstage, to Mathieu*) Take a grip of yourself, m'sieur. You will kindly answer the question!
Mathieu Ugh! Yes ... I s ... s ... s ... at the Fr ... Fr ... Fr ... Tr ... (*he moves to Paillardin and grabs him by the lapels*) Ho ... Ho ... Ho ...

Boucard moves R, UL *of the armchair*

Paillardin Come along now. It's not funny!
Pinglet (*aside*) He's stuttering well today! (*He rises and stands at the* R *end of the chaise*)

Mme Pinglet grabs Mathieu and shakes him, then gives up and pushes him behind her towards the desk. She makes a gesture of resignation to Paillardin

Mme Pinglet Monsieur Mathieu, you're doing this on purpose.

Mathieu At the Ho ... Ho ... Ho ... Ho ...! (*He gives a great kick, hitting Mme Pinglet on the bottom*)

Paillardin We'll never get it out of him.

Mme Pinglet goes flying onto the chaise

Pinglet, who was leaning against the chaise, is sent flying into Boucard, stamping on his toe

Boucard (*moving downstage a pace*) I've had a little idea ...

All An idea?

Boucard A solution to this difficult case! He can make a written statement!

Paillardin ⎫
           (*together*) Yes, yes. So he can! A written statement!
Mme Pinglet ⎭

Pinglet moves behind the armchair as Boucard moves DL *and seats Mathieu at the desk*

Mme Pinglet rises and moves to the R *of Mathieu*

Boucard Now. Sit you down, m'sieur. (*He takes out a paper and a pen*) And just write out your evidence.

Paillardin moves downstage behind Mathieu

Tell us exactly who you saw.

Mathieu I s ... s ... s ...

Maxime enters UR, *closes the door and moves between the chaise and the armchair, his hat in his hand*

Marcelle (*to Pinglet*) We're finished, Pinglet!

Pinglet We're cooked!

Paillardin ⎫
Boucard ⎬ (*together*) Go on! Go on! Write it down!
Mme Pinglet ⎭

Pinglet, having heard the door close, moves upstage to inspect it

Maxime What a lot of people! (*Aside*) Oh, my God! It's the fellow from last night. (*He puts his hat over his face*) If he recognizes me it's all up!

Maxime turns to the door to flee but sees Pinglet there. In haste he moves to the banister above the chaise, where Pinglet's bag is

Mathieu sees him and tries to rise, pointing his arm at Maxime but Mme Pinglet pushes it down twice. Mathieu then tries to rise but Boucard seats him firmly, again twice. Mathieu shakes his leg and raises his R *arm and yet again Mme Pinglet pushes it down*

Maxime takes a napkin and puts it over his head, then puts the bag over the napkin and his hat on top and staggers towards the stairs

Pinglet (*turning and seeing Maxime*) Stop thief!

Paillardin moves to Maxime and catches him at the bottom of the stairs

Boucard Excuse me, m'sieur. (*He rushes after Paillardin*) That's my job!

Boucard takes hold of Maxime's R arm and Paillardin his L and march him R of the chaise

Mme Pinglet moves to L of the chaise

Open up, m'sieur. (*He takes Maxime's hat off and knocks on the bag*) We all know you're in there!

Maxime (*struggling*) Leave me in peace. I'm not doing any harm.

Boucard }
Paillardin } (*together*) Take off that thing! Take it off!

Maxime No! No! Let me alone!

Paillardin pulls the bag off his head and dumps it through the banisters

Boucard pulls the napkin off

All Maxime!

Boucard (*seeing the soot on the napkin and on Maxime's face*) That's the individual!

All Who?

Boucard The male person I saw covered in soot. (*He puts the hat back on Maxime's head*)

All Maxime! It was Maxime!

Pinglet quickly moves to the L of his wife

Paillardin You young scoundrel! Was it you?

Maxime I have no idea what you're all talking about. (*He takes his hat off*)

Boucard The charge is ... you were the fellow at the Free Trade Hotel. Found in a compromising position.

Maxime How did you know?

All It was Maxime!

Mme Pinglet moves above the chaise

Pinglet Did you hear? Did you hear? He confessed!

Mathieu (*standing*) B ... b ... b ... but ... I s ... s ... s ...

Pinglet (*hitting Mathieu on the shoulder and forcing him to sit*) Shut up!

Mme Pinglet (*to Maxime*) Young man! I don't suppose you'll dare to suggest that you were up to monkey business with me?

Maxime With you? God forbid!

Boucard So who was it? I have a strong suspicion that the individual in question may have been of the female variety.

All A woman! You were with a woman. Who was it?

Maxime Oh, well then. Who cares? It was Victoire!

Paillardin Victoire? Victoire? Where is this Victoire?

Mme Pinglet In her room. She just went up to change.

Paillardin Leave this to me!

Paillardin moves to the door UR, opens it and goes into the hall

Paillardin (*off*) Victoire! Come down! You're wanted immediately! It's a matter of vital importance to us all!

Mathieu (*rising*) But I s ... s ... s ...

Pinglet (*pushing him down and swiping Mathieu on the head*) Oh, do shut up! No one else can get a word in edgeways!

Mathieu Very w ... w ...

Pinglet gives Mathieu a slap on the back which produces the word "well"

Well! (*He begins to write out his statement*)

Paillardin (*off*) Come along, my girl.

Victoire (*off*) But I haven't finished dressing!

Paillardin enters and moves DR

Victoire follows, dressed in Marcelle's puce dress

All The puce dress!

Mme Pinglet Where on earth did you get that dress?

Victoire It's just a dress. (*She moves* L *of Marcelle, who determinedly looks in the opposite direction*) I was trying it on. It was given to me by ...

Pinglet (*to Victoire*) Quiet, girl! Don't bother us with long explanations.

Mathieu continues writing

Paillardin (*moving* UR) So *you* were at the Free Trade Hotel last night!

Victoire Oh, m'sieur! However did you guess?

Mme Pinglet And you had the cheek to borrow my name!

Victoire I did what?

Pinglet No explanations! I told you. (*He moves upstage to Victoire*) We're all bored with explanations! Off you go now! We've heard quite enough from you! (*He pushes her towards the door*)

Mme Pinglet But, my dear ...

Mathieu folds up his statement

Pinglet And we've heard quite enough from you too. Thank you! (*To Victoire*) I thought I told you to go. Stop hanging about like yesterday's lunch.

Victoire But you wanted me!

Pinglet And now we don't want you any more! (*He pushes her nearer the door*)

Victoire Make up your mind!

Pinglet pushes Victoire out of the door and closes it

Mathieu (*holding up his statement to Boucard*) My sta ... sta ... sta ...

Mme Pinglet takes the statement but Pinglet snatches it from her as she is unfolding it and tears it up

Pinglet Your statement? Well, we shan't be needing that now! Now we know exactly what happened. We don't need your statement at all! Quite unnecessary!

All Quite unnecessary!

Mathieu (*in disappointment*) Oh!

Pinglet (*looking at his watch*) Look at the time! Quick! (*He pushes Mathieu downstage of the chaise to the door*) You'll miss your train back to Dieppe!
All The train to Dieppe!
Mathieu But I s ... s ... s ... Damn the rain!
Pinglet But it's sunny in Dieppe! Off you go!

Pinglet and Paillardin lift Mathieu up and throw him out. Pinglet shuts the door

All Off you go!

They move back into the room in relief

Mme Pinglet sits DL. *Paillardin sits in the armchair. Maxime sits on the chaise*

Pinglet Thank God that's over!
Boucard (*moving* R *of the chaise, to Maxime*) Well, young man. I don't think you'll be hearing any more about last night. Allow me to return your five thousand francs to you. Just count it, will you? (*He gives him the the money*)

Pinglet moves above the chaise and watches in horror

Marcelle moves downstage to UR *of the armchair*

Maxime To me?
Pinglet (*aside*) Ouch! He's giving him my five thousand francs!
Maxime (*counting the money*) *My* five thousand francs?
Boucard Of course.
Maxime Why did you give it to *me*?
Boucard Because you were the man committing the immoral act at the Free Trade Hotel.
Maxime Do they give you prizes for it? What a hotel! I'll go back there again.

CURTAIN

FURNITURE AND PROPERTY LIST

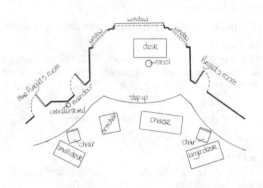

ACT I

On stage: Large white trestle table. *On it:* papers, plans, ruler, T-square, various
    pens and pencils, a directory
High stool
Chest of drawers. *On it:* samples of tiles and stone
Large work table. *On it:* books, rolled-up plans, blotter, pen, inkstand, a
    pot of flowers
Mirror
Shelf. *On it:* rolled-up plans
Sofa
Small writing desk. *On it:* cigarettes, lighter. *In it:* key
Portfolio
Clock
Bell-pull
Framed plans
Tinted drawings
Plaster models of cornices and ornamental mouldings
Armchair
3 chairs
Umbrella stand. *In it:* Mme Pinglet's umbrella
Sideboard. *On it:* book. *In it:* key

Window seat. *In it:* rope ladder
Palm tree in pot

Off stage: Coat, hat, bag, goggles **(Mme Pinglet)**
Salver. *On it:* a card **(Victoire)**
Tray. *On it:* dinner for one **(Victoire)**

Personal: **Mme Pinglet:** 2 samples of material
Marcelle: handkerchief
Pinglet: jacket, money, hat
Maxime: book, spectacles
Victoire: salver. *On it:* some letters
Mathieu: wet coat, umbrella, hat, bag, gloves, jacket, money, pencil
Porter: massive trunk
4 porters: one trunk each in descending size
Violette: umbrella, shoulder bag
Marguerite: umbrella, shoulder bag, book
Paquerette: umbrella, shoulder bag, lolly
Pervenchie: umbrella, shoulder bag, rag doll

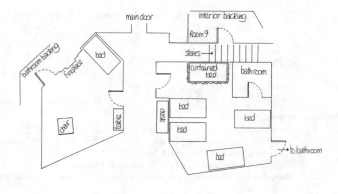

ACT II

Strike: All

Set: 2 small round tables with faded covers
Bed coverd with an eiderdown and surrounded by chintz curtains
2 straw-seated chairs
Clock
Globe
2 candlesticks
2 vases with artificial flowers
Bedside table. *On it:* jug, glass, sugar-bowl
Board with hanging keys
Small table with drawers. *On it:* candlesticks, one lit, candles, drill. *In it:*
     key
4 iron bedsteads
Small mirror
3 chairs
Wooden bed with white curtains
Curtain hook
Bedside table
2 gas burners
Picture
Coal skuttle

Off stage: Tray. *On it:* teapot, cups, saucers, spirit-lamp, kettle, sugar-bowl holding
     sugar lumps **(Boulot)**
Tray. *On it:* cups **(Boulot)**
2 chairs **(Boulot)**
4 chairs **(The four sisters)**
Hot water-bottle **(Boulot)**
Hot water-bottle **(Pinglet)**
4 nightlights **(Violette)**

Personal: **Ernest:** hat, cane
Chervet: cane with curved handle
Paillardin: hat, small bag holding silk nightshirt, book, combs, brushes,
     slippers, and a de-luxe cigar box
Pinglet: enormous cigar, Marcelle's bag, hat, jacket
Marcelle: hat, puce coloured dress, handkerchief, bag containing a lace
     mantilla
Mathieu: umbrella, bag, hat, coat, small cigar in pocket
Violette: ⎫
Marguerite: ⎬ umbrella, bag containing night attire
Paquerette: ⎭
Pervenchie: umbrella, bag containing night attire, doll
Maxime: book, hat
Victoire: umbrella, hat, jacket
Boucard: umbrella

ACT II

Strike: All

Set: As for Act I
        Napkin and water on tray
        Pinglet's bag near the banister

Off stage: Salver. *On it:* some letters **(Victoire)**
          Salver. *On it:* one letter **(Victoire)**
          Smelling salts **(Paillardin)**
          Marcelle's puce dress **(Victoire)**

Personal: **Pinglet:** hat, jacket, dressing gown, spectacles, smoking jacket, boot minus
          a button
          Maxime: hat, cigarette
          Victoire: telegram
          Mme Pinglet: torn dress, hat, coat, umbrella
          Mathieu: hat, coat
          Boucard: umbrella, gloves, hat, notebook, spectacles, five thousand francs

LIGHTING PLOT

Property fittings required: 2 gas burners

Interior. An apartment. Interior of an hotel

ACT I

To open: Full general lighting

No cues

ACT II

To open: Rooms L and R in darkness, landing lit by 2 gas burners only

Cue 1	**Bastien:** "Most of our clients prefer the dark." *Subdued lights up on stairs*	(Page 28)
Cue 2	**Bastien:** ". . . he'll have got used to it." *Subdued lights up on hall and landing*	(Page 29)
Cue 3	**Paillardin** "Lead on, to the haunted chamber!" *Subdued lights up on* L *bedroom*	(Page 32)
Cue 4	**Paillardin** goes into the bathroom *Black-out* L *bedroom*	(Page 34)
Cue 5	**Pinglet:** "Perfect." *Subdued lights up on* R *bedroom*	(Page 34)
Cue 6	**Bastien** exits to the hall *Subdued lights up on* L *bedroom*	(Page 35)
Cue 7	**Paillardin** walks into the hall *Black-out* L *bedroom*	(Page 35)
Cue 8	**Mathieu:** "Lead us to it." *Subdued lights up on* L *bedroom*	(Page 41)
Cue 9	**Marcelle** takes the candle into the bathroom *Black-out* R *bedroom*	(Page 49)
Cue 10	**Marcelle** emerges from the bathroom *Subdued lights up on* R *bedroom*	(Page 49)
Cue 11	**Mathieu** goes out onto the landing *Black-out* L *bedroom*	(Page 50)
Cue 12	**Mathieu** moves into his bedroom *Subdued lights up on* L *bedroom*	(Page 51)
Cue 13	**Mathieu** exits to his bathroom *Black-out* L *bedroom*	(Page 51)

Cue 14	**Paillardin** goes into the room on the L *Subdued lights up on* L *bedroom*	(Page 53)
Cue 15	**Victoire** pulls **Maxime** into room nine *Black-out the landing*	(Page 55)
Cue 16	**Pervenchie:** "Butter fingers!" *Subdued lights up on landing*	(Page 56)
Cue 17	**Mathieu:** "It's a woman." *Black-out* L *bedroom*	(Page 58)
Cue 18	**Maxime:** "Victoire!" *Subdued lights up on* L *bedroom*	(Page 58)
Cue 19	**All:** "To the police station!" *The lights fade to black-out on the last note of music*	(Page 64)

ACT III

To open: Full general lighting

No cues

EFFECTS PLOT

ACT I

Cue 1   As Curtain rises   (Page 1)
            Gentle rain

Cue 2   Pinglet emerges on his knees from behind the chaise   (Page 22)
            Rain stops

Cue 3   **Pinglet:** "Always keep a spare in the desk."   (Page 26)
            Sound of bolt being drawn

ACT II

Cue 4   **Bastien:** ". . .thirty years he'll have got used to it."   (Page 29)
            Sound of bell ringing

Cue 5   **Bastien:** "And all free, gratis, and for nothing!"   (Page 32)
            Sound of bell ringing

Cue 6   **Bastien:** "It's a little nest of enchantment."   (Page 32)
            Sound of bell ringing

Cue 7   **Bastien** is about to sit at the desk   (Page 52)
            Sound of bell ringing

ACT III

Cue 8   As Act III opens   (Page 65)
            Clock strikes seven

Cue 9   **Pinglet:** "Shoot the bolt."   (Page 72)
            Sound of bolt closing

Cue 10   **Mathieu:** ". . . I saw quite clearly . . ."   (Page 87)
            Sound of a thunder clap, then pouring rain

MADE AND PRINTED IN GREAT BRITAIN BY
LATIMER TREND & COMPANY LTD PLYMOUTH

MADE IN ENGLAND